Life in Alien Territory

Memories of Peace Corps Service in Mali

Life in Alien Territory: Memories of Peace Corps Service in Mali

Published by Wheatmark®
1760 East River Road, Suite 145, Tucson, Arizona 85718 U.S.A.
www.wheatmark.com

ISBN: 978-162787-179-2 (paperback)
ISBN: 978-162787-180-8 (ebook)
LCCN: 2014946151

Life in Alien Territory

Memories of Peace Corps Service in Mali

Renate A. Schulz

Proceeds from the sale of this book will be donated to support Peace Corps projects in West Africa.

For Sigrid, Peter,
Hannah and Michael

Contents

Preface xiii
Political Map of Africa xv
Mali Information...xvii
Dedication xxi

Part I : Grandma goes to Africa

Departure 3
Leaving familiar territory 4
Getting ready for life in alien territory 6

Part II: Pre-Service Training

New home sweet home 11
Dear Congressman 13
Mansa Musa's Revenge... 15
I've had it!...16
R & R..17
Teaching an old dog new tricks 18
How not to treat your mother 20
Escape to "la vie à l'américaine"................................21

There must be a better way!...................................22

Ebola?...24

A bloody mess 26

Mohamed 27

Daily routine 28

It's the culture, stupid! 30

Adjustment..31

Peace Corps 1963 vs. Peace Corps 2011...............33

Culture shock in retrospect............................34

Fourth of July 36

Reading, writing, 'rithmetic 37

The meaning of statistics................................41

Peace Corps impact on village life 43

Preparation for life at our work-sites 46

A first taste of Bamako 51

Return to "the bush" 61

Campement Kangaba................................68

Farewell to Kobalakoro................................70

End of training..74

Taking the "oath of office" 75

Photos 82

Part III: Peace Corps Service

Getting oriented..93

Shopping Malian style.....................................94

Reflections on Islam 96

Another move..100

A Sunday outing...101

The honeymoon is over 103

The end of Ramadan...106

Cholera 108

Life of the middle class 109

How to scare small children 112

Trip to Dogon Country 113

Mopti 124

Back "home" 127

First faculty meeting 128

Introduction to the English Language Club 131

A tale of dirty sheets 133

A visit to a primary school 136

A smart thief 138

Official start of semester 144

Kafka revisited! 146

The life of a working stiff 150

Looking for new digs 153

A visit to the U.S. Embassy 154

A moving experience 156

My new living quarters 159

The tale of the forged CFA bill 162

A pleasant week-end 163

The life of a working stiff, continued 164

Of Cuban-American friendship 168

Tabaski 169

Impenetrable cultural secrets 174

A visit 175

Am I losing it?—Part One 178

Back in Tubaniso 182

Open, Sesame! 183

Corruption 186

Thanksgiving 188

How to become rich and famous................................190

Good help is hard to get.......................................191

All that jazz 194

Midterm 196

Reverse culture shock 200

Back in "Allah's country".....................................204

How not to run a language fair................................206

Adjusted?..210

End-of-semester chaos...211

A paint job..213

Chaos continues 214

Trouble in River City 215

Harmattan 220

A Malian wedding...220

Am I losing it? Part II 227

Life as a roadie 229

An ode to Bamako taxi drivers 238

Open Sesame! Episode #2..240

Open Sesame! Episode #3..242

Living high on the hog...243

Two major victories 247

Part IV: The end

Off to spring break in Ghana 253

The coup 255

Stranded in Accra..260

Evacuation...265

* * *

Epilogue 269

Acknowledgements 273

Glossary...275

Suggested Readings..................................279

Preface

THIS JOURNAL, DIVIDED into 93 entries, chronicles my experiences, observations, impressions, reflections, challenges, frustrations, philosophical meanderings and self-searchings during eleven months of service (June 2011—April 2012) in the U.S. Peace Corps in Mali, West Africa, before the Peace Corps was evacuated from that country due to a military coup d'état. Some names have been changed to protect the privacy of individuals.

Like many friends with whom I shared my journal entries during my time in Mali, the reader may question why I was putting myself through this "boot camp" ordeal of on-site Peace Corps training and of working in the African hinterlands at seventy-plus years of age. I have to admit that I asked myself that same question on numerous occasions!

A year or so after retirement from my professorial position at the University of Arizona, after completing all unfinished commitments left over after almost thirty years of working at that institution, I came to the conclusion that I needed something larger than myself to devote energies to. Come evening, I frequently realized that I had done absolutely nothing that was of use to anyone except to those where I spent my money.

I could, of course, have found some local volunteer activities to provide me with a sense of purpose and accomplishment. But most volunteer activities I explored were too restrictive as to the time commitment required, and none offered travel and adventure. Also, I was sort of frustrated with my own U.S. culture that certainly has the knowledge, expertise as well as financial and technical resources to solve many of its own problems but that lacks the political will and resolve to do so. Thus, remembering my first Peace Corps experience in Nigeria (1963-1965) and the formative, life-changing effect it had on me, I decided to re-join that organization for a 27-months stint in Mali, West Africa. Well, if I was looking for something larger and more important than myself to devote my energies to, I certainly had arrived at the right place!

Political Map of Africa

Mali Information

THE FOLLOWING INFORMATION was gleaned from various handouts based on U.S. State Department and Peace Corps publications. Depending on the source, numbers reported often conflict. All figures are estimates.

Location: West Africa—ranging from Saharan/sub-Saharan savannah (65%) to tropical surroundings; land-locked; bordered by Algeria, Niger, Burkino Faso, Côte d'Ivoire, Guinea, Senegal and Mauritania.

Capital city: Bamako—around 1.8 million inhabitants.

Size: Approximately the size of Texas and California combined.

Size of population: Between 12 and 13 million.

Life expectancy: 49–54 years (depending on source); about half of population is under 14!!!! Estimated population increase per year over three percent; predicted population increase for all of Africa by 2020 is 23% (Source: *Les Afriques*, No. 170, p. 3.) Get ready for future unemployment, unrest, famine, wars and revolutions!

Literacy rate: 31%; 64% of children (predominantly boys) attend primary school at least through second grade.

Per capita annual income (estimated 2006): US$ 470. Annual skilled worker salary: $1,560. (For comparison, my monthly base subsistence allowance as Peace Corps Volunteer living in the capital city was around US$320.)

Government: Before the military coup on March 21, 2012, Mali presented itself as a multi-party, democratic (universal suffrage), secular, decentralized republic. The country had been fairly stable between 1992 and 2012, but there were active Al Qaeda cells (AQIM or Al Qaeda in the Islamic Mahgreb) and a Tuareg separatist movement in the northern part of Mali (including Timbuktu). Beginning in early 2012, the north of Mali (Gao, Kidal and Timbuktu regions) was practically controlled by militant Islamists.

Religion: 90% Moslem, 4% Christian, remainder animist.

Ethnic groups and languages: 317 ethnic groups with over 50 living languages: e.g., Mande (Bambara, Malinke, Soninke) 52%; smaller percentages of Fulani, Dogon, Songhai, Tuareg, Senufo, Bobo, Bozo, Maurs, etc.

Official national language: French (spoken fluently by fewer than 20% of the population).

Economy: Mali is among the three poorest countries in the world, together with Niger and Mauritania. Subsistence farming (millet, sorghum, corn, peanuts, rice, okra, cotton), nomadic herding (cattle, goats), river fishing—86%. **Export:** Cotton, gold. **Imports:** most everything apart from food—mostly from China.

Currency: CFA (Communauté Financière Africaine). West and Central African currency used by all former French African colonies.

Climate: hot, hotter, damn hot, and hot and humid. Temperatures of 113 degree Fahrenheit or 45 degree Centigrade are no exception! (Think Phoenix in August without air conditioning—year-round.)

Gender equity and human development: According to a 2006 UN Human Development Report, Mali ranks 175th of 177 nations on the gender development index, measuring the gap in literacy, wealth, power, etc. between men and women. Newsweek's 2011 Global Women's Progress Report, using a 0-100-point scale to measure factors, such as Justice, Health, Education, Economics and Politics ranked Mali fifth of 165 countries with an overall score of 17.6. Wikipedia ranks Mali 182nd out of 187 on the UN Human Development Index.

History: The golden age of Malian Empires began in 1230 with the powerful king Sundiata and ended with the Moroccan invasion in 1591. Much of what is now Mali was on major caravan and trade routes from

North Africa and the Mediterranean, transporting gold, salt, and slaves. Timbuktu (Tombouctou) was an early Islamic center of learning and trade. French colonization (as part of the French Soudan) began in the 1890s. As most colonial powers, the French drew the country's boundaries without regard to ethnicity or tribe, language and culture of those colonized, the cause of many of the current conflicts in West Africa (e.g., in Nigeria, Ivory Coast, Liberia, Congo, etc.). Mali gained its national independence from France in 1960.

Dedication

I DEDICATE THIS book to the people of Mali whose paths I crossed, who were my students, colleagues, neighbors and friends. They welcomed me without reservation, protected me, generously shared what they had, and were patient with my impatience, tolerant of my lack of tolerance, and taught me that poverty does not mean unhappiness or lack of joy; that modernization does not necessarily have to mean westernization; and that one can live—and indeed thrive—without rushing from one commitment or entertainment to the next, and without being bombarded by constant advertising and an over-choice of unnecessaries.

May Mali regain its status as a "model of emerging West African democracy" which guarantees equal rights and fair law enforcement to all of its citizens, regardless of their gender or ethnic or religious backgrounds. May the Malian people succeed in improving their lives, particularly that of women and children in providing educational opportunities to all boys and girls. May they find ways to discourage—among other scourges—corruption, nepotism, forced early marriages and female genital mutilation. May they find food, housing, health care and employment opportunities for their burgeoning population without losing their commitment to family, respect for their elders, and without falling prey to "westernization" and its hurried life style, rampant consumerism and greed.

Part I   *Grandma goes to Africa*

Africa has parasites so particular and diverse as to occupy every niche of the body: intestines small and large, the skin, the bladder, the male and female reproductive tracts, interstitial fluids, even the cornea.... If God had amused himself inventing the lilies of the field, he surely knocked His own socks off with the African parasites.

—Barbara Kingsolver, *The Poisonwood Bible*

Departure

June 1

THERE I AM, with 23 young, bright-eyed and exuberant Americans (13 females, 11 males), in a conference room of the Holiday Inn, Georgetown, receiving our departure briefing for Peace Corps Mali, West Africa. Those assembled—in appearance and last names—reflect the marvelous mixture of what is America. Most hyphenated Americans are represented in the group, with the possible exception of a "Native American." I am the token senior citizen. I could be everybody's grandmother. My fellow idealists and world improvers are all under 30, the majority just—or at most two years—out of college. Our group will be working in two different sectors in Mali: education and water/sanitation.

We review the Peace Corps mission, the core expectations for Peace Corps Volunteers, medical issues, and logistics for departure.

We prepare skits to simulate what to do and what not to do in certain situations, keeping in mind possible points of cultural conflicts.

And, in small groups, we discuss our fears, anxieties and aspirations. Mostly we remain on the topic of fears and anxieties: snakes, scorpions, bugs, terrorists, rape and sexual harassment, theft, gender role difficulties, strange foods and food safety, race/ethnicity issues, religious conflicts, illness, sanitation/hygiene, western-style toilets (or the lack thereof), AIDS, boredom, loneliness, etc.

In the evening the group goes out for one last night in familiar territory to blow their $140 per diem and travel money. I am invited to come along, but decide to stay in the hotel and get annoyed by TV commercials interrupted by scenes of violence.

Leaving familiar territory
June 2 and 3

THE NEXT DAY the group assembles with their luggage in the hotel lobby, and we leave by bus shortly after noon for the Department of Health, Education and Welfare, where—after our first of several metal screenings of the day—we are getting our Yellow Fever shots.

We continue on to Dulles International around 2 p.m. to wait for the 9:55 p.m. departure. Because of the Peace Corps staff's previous bad experiences with airheaded volunteers, who lost their official government passports or World Health cards between the hotel and the airport, we are not given our official travel documents before check-in time around 7 p.m., so the group needs to stay together. Annoying!

* * *

Long, rough, miserable flight from D.C. to Paris on Air France. I can't sleep. At least Air France is serving Champagne. We arrive on June 3, shortly after 11 a.m. Paris time and have to wait until 4:15 p.m. for the connecting flight to Mali.

*** * *

There is mounting excitement as we approach Bamako and experience the usual third-world chaos upon landing. Peace Corps Mali staff is at the airport in full force, welcoming us, helping with our luggage, and loading humans into a mini-bus and luggage onto a truck for the hour-long ride to Tubaniso, an agricultural education center, made available to the Peace Corps for training purposes by the government of Mali.

* * *

Arrival at Tubaniso around 11 p.m. Major culture shock! Our accommodations consist of small, round, thatched-roofed huts, equipped with nothing but three rusty, steel-framed, mosquito-net-covered, single beds. My two roommates and I barely have enough space to cram in our luggage.

The toilets are under the stars: several cemented holes in the ground surrounded by tin shacks. The adjoining showers are equally luxurious. One of the experienced volunteers who is part of the welcoming committee demonstrates how best to hit the toilet hole to avoid major clean up after you do "your business." Some of my young colleagues without third-world travel experience are in visible shock.

In spite of the open door and the creaking ceiling fan, our little hut is unbearably hot. But we are all exhausted and fall asleep soon after hitting the hard pillows long after midnight.

Getting ready for life in alien territory

June 4

GLORIOUS COOL SHOWERS in cement stalls that are threatened with a takeover by termites. By the time I'm dressed I could use another shower. For breakfast we negotiate the unpaved, pot-hole infested road to the so-called *refectoire*—a large, brick, warehouse-like structure, equipped with basic steel furniture whose plastic table coverings clearly have seen better days. Breakfast consists of soft French bread, butter, jam, locally made peanut butter and Nescafe or Lipton's.

After breakfast, in a large, thatch-covered open-air structure, we are officially introduced to the Peace Corps staff who count more than our small group of 24 trainees. Most of the staff are Malian citizens, locally employed. Only the top of the Peace Corps Mali bureaucratic hierarchy consists of American nationals. We are provided with training sessions covering health issues, security, language learning, transportation, use of drugs and alcohol (DON'T!), appropriate behavior for gays or lesbians (GO BACK INTO THE CLOSET!). We are individually tested for our French language proficiency. Although I have not used French for more than twenty years I receive a rating of "superior." I suspect that my non-American French accent got them fooled -☺

We will stay in Tubaniso until next Wednesday, when

we are farmed out to live with families in various near-by villages. We are warned not to expect an improvement in the area of sanitation or bodily comforts, but we are promised our own rooms or huts.

Part II *Pre-Service Training*

[The] strong interdependence of family is…
one of the most seductive features of the Malian
culture: We have nothing like it anymore. So long
as there remains on earth a single aunt or uncle,
grandparent, grandchild, cousin, or second cousin,
no Malian is ever permitted to live alone, or to be
sick alone, or to die alone.

And yet, in the extreme with which it is practiced here, this family closeness is also a formi-
dable obstacle to democratic development, for
it encourages one of the most resistant forms of
corruption. Nepotism. A Malian with a good job
is not only forgiven for favoring his relatives with
appointments and promotions, he is expected to
do so and considered disloyal if he doesn't.

—Donald Lawder,
Fishing in the Sky:
The Education of Namory Keita

New home sweet home

June 8

OH, MY GOD! Dear Jesus! Allah, the infinitely good and merciful! or whoever else is in charge here! Can I really do this for the next two months? This morning I arrived in Kobalakoro, a village about 20 km (one hour drive) from Bamako, on the paved road to Segou, my on-site training station.

Our sub-group of seven volunteers housed in Kobala-koro were welcomed warmly by the villagers awaiting our van near the local market. Accompanied by a drummer and many children who fought over who could carry our luggage, we were led to the house of the *dugutigi* (village chief) where our host families awaited us. As is customary here, all the volunteers were given Malian names, based on their host family affiliation, and we were led to our new place of residence. My new name is Salimata Diarra.

I have a small, bare "room" in the compound of the *dugutigi's* nephew, Boubakar Diarra, his wife Aissata Touré, his three children (2, 6, and 8 years of age), his mother, three helpers, one donkey, and umpteen chickens—all sharing the small courtyard right in front of my room. The sole piece of furniture supplied in my cemented cubicle is a rusty steel bed with a dirty mattress. There also is a plastic prayer mat.

Using my metal hip as excuse, I sit on a low, partly broken lawn chair while eating on a lower-yet, small, uneven table under the single tree that provides some shade in the infernal humid heat in the courtyard. I share a bowl of rice and sauce (actually quite tasty) with Aissata, while her husband shares a bowl with the children separately on the ground.

Tomorrow I'll try to find a spoon to use while eating. This eating by hand is definitely not for me, particularly since my host family members do not appear to have acquired the habit of hand washing before a meal. Furthermore, I can't get anything into my mouth without spilling the stew all over myself.

My room with its tin roof is incredibly hot. The children permit no privacy whatsoever. The entire neighborhood seems to be here. Theoretically, the open door and opposite small, glass-less window giving out to a dusty village path should provide some air. But between the screaming children, the sonorous voice of the muezzin's five-times-daily call to prayer over the nearby mosque's loudspeaker, the braying donkey (the animal sounds as if it were suffocating), and the constant traffic of villagers who get their water supply at the village pump right next to my compound, there is mostly dust, a fetid smell from the nearby toilet sink hole, and a cacophony of noise that comes through the window.

Communication with my host family members is very limited, particularly when my host, Boubakar,—the only one in the compound who speaks French—is not around. Aissata, his wife, understands some French, but I can't understand anything she says. Fanta, the eight-year old, had one or two years of primary instruction, supposedly conducted in French, but her linguistic competence is limited to "bonjour," "merci," and "comment allez-vous?" Oh yes, she can also count in French and sing a mangled version of "Frère Jaques."

Dear Congressman...

June 9

My host family members are trying hard to communicate with me, feed me, and supply me with buckets of water for multiple daily "baths." The constant flow of people from the extended family who come to greet me wears me out.

This must be similar to what European village life was like in the Middle Ages or even earlier—except, of course, for the ubiquitous plastic trash, the occasional TV antenna, and zippers: dirt roads, a village well, mud walls, primitive outhouses (holes in the floor) leading their waste water into standing water pits outside the compound walls, animals (goats, donkeys, chickens) running around freely, filthy, near-naked children, donkey carts as major means of transportation.

I realize on an intellectual level that I am suffering from major culture shock. I feel paralyzed but cannot rationally overcome it. I am angry at the Peace Corps for expecting us to live in these conditions. Jesus, how difficult or expensive could it be to supply us with a table and chair and some shelves or a bench to get at least our medications and toilet articles off the floor? How difficult could it be to clean up the concession where we have classes, and supply some surfaces on which to put our books and notebooks, instead of having to put them on the ground littered with chicken shit, greasy papers, and plastic bags blowing around in the wind?

Dammit, does no one at Peace Corps Bamako realize that American senior citizens do not have bladders like college grads, and that they should not be expected to fight aggressive cockroaches on their nightly visits to the toilet?

I am so frustrated that I consider writing to my Congressman to complain about my placement. Thank God, I am still lucid enough to realize the ridiculousness of this idea. If I can't cut it, all I have to do is to call the Peace Corps office in Bamako on my cell phone and request to be sent home. Those who made that call in the past were whisked out of the country within 48 hours.

I am also frustrated with my language learning experience. I am too old for this type of intensive, repeat-and-memorize language learning! I can't remember a damn thing and am clearly the slowest Bambara learner of the group. I am tempted to quit. I talk to Mohamed and Alassane, my language and culture facilitators, who try to encourage me and tell me "to move at my own pace." That is easier said than done when one is 50 years older than the rest of the students. It is clear that I am slowing down my class mates and wasting valuable time.

* * *

I experience the first storm of the rainy season.

The violence of the rain reminds me of Arizona. My compound is a muddy lake until evening. Thank God there is a break in the heat, but rising humidity and increasing hordes of flies.

It seems to me that the entire village population is watching a soccer game on a small, black and white TV run by a car battery in front of my room. The heat is unbearable. I am bathed in sweat and can't sleep. I take off my night gown and try to sleep in the buff under my mosquito net, hoping that none of the people right outside my door will decide to aim their flashlight directly into my room. Even if they do, I no longer care!

Mansa Musa's Revenge
(known in Mexico as Moctezuma's Revenge)

June 10

I DON'T THINK there is one even surface in my compound. Definitely not in the *njegen* (bathroom/toilet) where my soap falls down from the wall separating the toilet enclosure from the courtyard (no door). I dry off, put back on my moo-moo, retrieve my soap and re-start the complicated washing/juggling process to keep soap, towel, etc. off the *njegen* floor.

You have not really lived until you have diarrhea and are trying to hit a Malian toilet hole! I use up my roll of toilet paper trying to wipe away the damage. Pretty hopeless, since the cement surface is very rough. Even several *selidagas* (plastic tea kettles) full of water don't wash away the damage completely. Embarrassed by my ineptitude, I leave it to my host "mother" to clean up what is left.

It doesn't help that the grandmothers of my and the neighboring *dugutigi*'s compound (both somewhat younger than I) walk around topless in the evening. I am quite certain that the Peace Corps does not expect me to "go native" on that custom. . . . It appears that breasts are not considered to be sexual symbols in this part of the world, but don't you dare to show any leg above the knee or all eyes will be on you!

* * *

I am simply not used to living so close to the ground. With the help of one of my host's "brothers" who speaks a semi-comprehensible version of French I order a small table and bench to be made by one of the local carpenters.

* * *

I can't sleep because of incredible heat. Am unable to work, read, review—even think straight. Again, I encounter dozens of giant cockroaches on my nightly visit to the *njegen* and am totally grossed out.

I've had it!

June 11

I WAKE UP with a heat rash and feel somewhat queasy. I have problems with the lengthy, daily, ritualized greeting and blessing routine I have memorized and have to go through with adult family members and anyone who stops by the compound. I thoroughly dislike this communal living and lack of privacy.

I have decided to throw in the towel unless the Peace Corps can find different living quarters for me and accommodate my age and language learning style. I talk to the assistant director of training (a Malian) who came to the village from Bamako together with an experienced volunteer to check on us. They promise to talk to the training director, and let me know of any possible alternative option(s).

R & R

Sunday, June 12

FREE DAY, NO classes. The entire group of Peace Corps trainees reunites at the language compound in my village. Much excitement for trainees as well as village children who follow everywhere we go! They touch our hair, hold our hands, examine our skin and clothes, and chatter away, trying to elicit the couple of phrases of Bambara we have learned. I love these smiling, beautiful children and I would so much like to hold or hug them, if they just were not so filthy!

My young colleagues decide to use the bicycles that were brought for us from Tubaniso to find a bar in a neighboring village. Our village has no bar, and furthermore, it would hurt our reputation and that of our Moslem host families if we were seen drinking alcoholic beverages.

I decide to return to my compound and sit outside

under the tree for the remainder of the day. I review some of the language material, do homework, and try to practice Bambara with my host family members. When I infer that my 22-year-old host "mother" had her first child at 12, I can't help but think of my 12-year-old granddaughter and become very perturbed. Later I find out that Aissata was actually 14 years old when she had her first child—somewhat, but not much better! Although the Malian constitution determines the age of adulthood at 18, in the villages it is not unusual to marry girls off at puberty—often to much older men.

What does it take to help change some of the cultural practices of traditional societies that impede their social, educational, human and economic development? Peace Corps Volunteers are supposed to function as community development agents. How can there be development without a drastic change in the role and rights of Malian women?

Teaching an old dog new tricks

June 14

WILL I EVER get used to people spitting two yards away from the little table where I sit, or doing their morning or evening ablutions in "public"?

I am slowly developing some survival strategies. I hung up some rope in my room to dry my towel and sweat-soaked nightgown. The carpenter delivered a contraption that gets my medications and cosmetic articles off the dirty cement floor. I thought I had requested a small table and bench, but what was delivered was a bulky, one-piece, school-desk-like contraption with a slanted table surface. The height of the supposed writing surface is totally out of proportion to the seat. When I sit on the bench, the writing surface starts at the level of my neck. I was too exhausted to ask the carpenter to re-do it.

I am using the toilet bucket supplied by the Peace Corps for a hand washing station and to keep the soap and shampoo off the *njegen* floor. The toilet bucket was to serve me during the night to avoid my pilgrimages to the *njegen*, but I simply could not face delivering my "night soil" to its final resting place by carrying it through the middle of the assembled residents of my compound.

I am no longer in Bambara class with the rest of my cohort, but am permitted to concentrate on reviewing my French by reading a novel by a French West African author (*Maimouna* by Abdulaye Sadji), writing summaries, and having periodic individual discussions with Mohamed. I feel relieved.

Trying to integrate myself into my host family is the hardest thing I ever had to do in my life. I am using it as a survival test. I am certain that once I am assigned to a working site and get my own place I will be able to adjust. I had few problems while I served in the Peace Corps in Nigeria. Of course, there I was much younger and had a husband as support system. I catch myself thinking of my ex-husband more now than I have in the past thirty years. I appreciate in retrospect his company and abilities as a handyman while living in the bush.

We lost our first trainee today. He decided that he

could not take village life and is being shipped home on the next available flight. We also have the first case of amoebas. The young woman is totally lethargic, has a high fever and diarrhea. She is shipped to the Peace Corps infirmary in Bamako to be dosed with antibiotics.

How not to treat your mother

June 16

THE PEACE CORPS training director was alerted by his assistant about my discontent and comes from Bamako to check on me. I try to tell him all that is bothering me, but don't think he understands the extent of my frustrations. He talks to my host family and suggests as solution to my sleep problems that I sleep outside on the ground on my plastic prayer mat, and fasten the mosquito net on the straw hangar that provides minimal shade between the two buildings in the compound. I look at him in disbelief. If I would follow his advice, that would leave about two yards on each side of my prayer mat for people to pass, not to mention that I would need to wait until the TV-watching villagers go home before going to sleep; and not to mention the early morning traffic, cooking and toilet activities within an arm's length of where I would be sleeping.

I know I am a bother and Peace Corps staff would like to get rid of the problem, but I strongly doubt that any of them would propose a similar solution for their own mothers. Definitely not the American staff! But they stay safely out of my reach in Bamako.

* * *

The next day, the program manager for the Peace Corps Education Program calls me from Bamako. He tells me that the (Malian) Peace Corps staff has discussed my situation with the (American) Country Director, but nothing could be done immediately. He asks me if I am able to survive another ten days until the group is to return for a three-day break to Tubaniso. I agree. Obviously, the Peace Corps has made an investment in me, and I have made an investment in the Peace Corps. I want this to work, but my resolution weakens by the hour.

Escape to "la vie à l'américaine"

June 19

WE ARE BACK in Tubaniso. It is amazing how perceptions become relativized in such a short time. Tubaniso with its neon tubes, ceiling fans, water faucets, shower heads, tables and chairs to eat and work on, as well as its relative cleanliness and possibility of clandestine trips to the one "real" toilet in the dispensary appear as luxury.

There is major excitement among my young colleagues! The Peace Corps vehicle picks us up for a visit to Bamako and the American Club to drink beer, eat pizza or hamburgers, and swim in the club's small pool. I meet three other older volunteers and am relieved that I am not the only one over 30. I am, however, the oldest volunteer in the country.

I also meet Jeremy, the volunteer teaching English at the public, university-level art institute specializing in dance, music, theater, the plastic arts and multi-media whom I am most likely to replace in August, provided I survive Peace Corps training. Jeremy assures me that I can do the job and that my accommodations would have many of the comforts I now lack.

In addition to sit-down toilets, the Bamako American Club has wireless. An email message from my Tucson neighbor informs me that my house in Tucson is being invaded by wasps through one of the skylights in the bathroom. Jesus! I can't deal with that now in addition to having to return to my fly-infested Malian village.

There must be a better way!

June 20 and 21

I'M BACK IN Kobalakoro. My namesake, the real Salimata Diarra, my host's sister, has arrived from Gao for a two-week visit. She is an attractive, well fed woman of around 40, with a marvelous wardrobe but limited French language skills. People come by the dozens to greet her. There is major commotion and lots of laughter throughout the day and much of the night. And, of course, it all happens right in front of my open door.

* * *

My village life strikes me as being surrealistic. I feel like I am residing in Garcia Marquez' *100 Years of Solitude.*

I question the Peace Corps' on-site training concept

that puts trainees immediately with the least developed segment of the Malian population. This immediate immersion in poverty, superstition, filth and lack of sanitation can color one's attitude toward the country and its people and inject a sense of hopelessness. I believe it would be wiser to put us with literate, educated Malians of the (admittedly tiny) emerging middle class with whom we would initially have more in common in terms of education, experience, life style, expectations and goals than with illiterate farmers. But then again, the majority of my young colleagues will actually have to work in village settings and it may be better that they experience the shock sooner than later.

I also believe that the Peace Corps is missing a great opportunity for informal education about cleanliness and sanitation in the walled concession where our classes are held. True, there is absolutely no infrastructure for garbage removal. But rather than sitting all day in the middle of blowing garbage, we could show—by example—how to set up a composting station for the degradable refuse; we could have a drum for paper and other refuse that could be burned weekly, and put the remaining stuff into a container to be eventually disposed of somehow. I am sure that by explaining our procedures and their rationale to the other residents living in the concession they would agree and cooperate with us and, perhaps, continue the practices after we are gone.

* * *

Hallelujah! My compound's recycling system (the

donkey's manure and garbage pile) is getting cleaned up. The refuse is brought by donkey cart to the fields as fertilizer. Unfortunately, this does not diminish the number of flies that surround me and my food.

Ebola?

June 22

I WAKE UP with a golf-ball-size swelling on top of my right foot. Major commotion! Everyone in the family plus the neighbors inspect the growth with great puzzlement. I have no pain, but call the Peace Corps Medical Office anyway. I am advised to wait it out for possible further symptoms. By evening the swelling has been absorbed by surrounding tissue, leaving only a slight tenderness in my foot. I will probably never know the cause of this affliction.

* * *

The instructional sessions on Malian cultural practices are the highlight of my days. Particularly interesting are the impenetrable kinship relationships. Regardless of who are the actual parents or how far removed the family link (if there is any at all), it seems everyone can claim a member of the younger generation as son or daughter. I don't believe the concept "cousin," nephew" or "niece" exists in traditional Malian society. They are all "brothers" or "sisters." Only the mother's siblings are referred to as "uncles" or "aunts. Very complicated!

Tradition dictates a hierarchical structure of responsibility for the members of a clan if anything happens to a father or mother. For instance, the older brother of the deceased husband apparently "inherits" the widow and her offspring.

Compared with western life styles that value the independent nuclear family, it is quite remarkable how Malians help support each other with their often very limited means. This may, in part, explain why Mali's largest share of foreign currency comes from Malian expatriates who live outside their country but nevertheless help support family and clan at home.

* * *

My diet continues to be limited. Breakfast: soft French bread with mayonnaise or locally made peanut butter, and tea. Lunch: boiled rice with a sauce containing a small gourd and a small piece of cabbage and sometimes a few pieces of tough meat (I like) or dried fish (I don't like). Dinner: French fries with a fried egg or pasta with an oily sauce, and tea. Whatever I leave on my plate is eaten by the children.

I avoid the nausea that I experienced initially by simply no longer watching Aissata heap food onto my plate that she has just rinsed in filthy dish water.

From the fit of my skirts I notice that I am losing weight. There may be some benefits to this experience after all!

* * *

I am now kind of living a life apart in the middle of

the family. Thank God, I am no longer the main attraction. I am occasionally ignored, even by visitors coming into the compound.

I have absolutely no news about the rest of the world. What is happening out there?????

A bloody mess

June 23

COMING INTO MY room from the *njegen* and the morning's bucket bath, I stumble, slip on the wet floor, fall, and hit my right cheek—just below the eye—on the famous contraption constructed by the local carpenter. Result: a two-inch gash with heavy bleeding. I guess the stream of blood is good for cleaning the wound.

I go to class anyway which today consists of an interesting session with a school management committee in a nearby school. The Peace Corps Education Program Assistant sees my face and immediately calls the medical office in Bamako to report the accident and my (by now) totally blood-shot and swollen right eye.

A Peace Corps vehicle takes me to Bamako through a phenomenal dust and rain storm. The huge red sand devils can easily compete with any sand storms Arizona has to offer. Assitou, the marvelous Malian nurse, cleans and bandages me, gives instructions on how to care for the wound, and, unfortunately, sends me back to Kobalakoro, where the entire village is one hell of a wet, muddy mess.

Mohamed

June 24

My conversations with Mohamed—intended to practice and improve my French—are the highlight of my days. I am reading novels by French West African authors and discuss my questions and impressions with him. He is a deeply religious (Moslem) and intelligent man, and though he has not yet had an opportunity to visit a "western" country, he tries to see issues from diverse perspectives.

So far, the novels I have read all deal with the impact of colonial rule on traditional values and practices, causing deep generational rifts between the young, who have received some schooling and speak the language of the colonial master, and their illiterate elders who continue to adhere to the practices, traditions, and superstitions of their ancestors.

* * *

I experienced my first hostility from a Malian today. On the way to the school concession, a man on a motorbike stopped me and asked whether I understood French and what I was doing in the village. Then he lit into me in beautiful French to tell me that Mali did not need the help of western countries or the U.S. Peace Corps, but needed to raise itself out of poverty within its own cultural context. Maybe he has a point.

* * *

Today I just made it home before a major rain storm. The tin roof over my bed started leaking. Thanks to Allah I was home to move the bed away from the drips.

Daily routine

June 25

MY EARLY MORNING routine: Around 5 a.m. it's still totally dark. I wake up when the muezzin makes three separate calls over the loudspeaker (very loud!). The prayer calls are in Arabic, the announcements are in Bambara. Unfortunately, I can't understand either. I quickly go to the *njegen* before anyone else comes out into the courtyard. Then I go back to my lumpy foam mattress, waiting for daylight.

Cocks start crowing and I hear faint calls to prayer from neighboring villages. The compound is slowly awakening, and the swish, swish, swish of the water pump near my window indicates that women or children are filling their plastic water buckets for the morning bath and breakfast.

Around 6 a.m., when it is slowly getting light and you no longer need a flashlight, I get out of bed. I tidy up my room and place my plastic water bucket outside my door to be filled by one of the children or helpers. Aissata has already lit the fire outside and has started to cook over the open flames. My host sits in front of my door on a low bench, performing his morning ablutions with his *selidaga* (plastic tea kettle full of water—no soap). The family avoids looking at me or saying anything, since it is not proper to greet people before you have washed yourself. I smile and wave at them and go to the *njegen* for my bucket bath.

Getting ready in the morning—which back home usually takes no longer than 20 minutes—takes me almost an hour. With no place to keep towel, clothes, soap, etc. off the dirty *njegen* floor, I still lack an efficient system for my morning bucket bath.

Returning to my room—freshly washed—I go through the elaborate traditional greeting routine practiced by Malians, which I have memorized, with the members of my family. Around seven o'clock I eat breakfast (tea, French bread with mayonnaise or peanut butter) and around 7:45 a.m. I leave for classes. Lunch is at 12:30 p.m.; resting time (or should I call it suffering-from-the-heat-time) lasts until 2:30 p.m.; back to class from 2:30–5 p.m.; dinner is anytime between 6 and 8 p.m.

I eat all my meals on a small, low, crooked table by myself, sitting on a dilapidated lawn chair in the court-yard. The rest of the family eats sitting on the ground. Lunch and dinner is usually the same for all members in the compound, while their breakfast is often different from mine, consisting of some kind of cereal paste which I have not yet had the courage to taste.

In the evening I usually go to bed around 8:30, after a bucket bath and after the last call to prayers. Quiet finally arrives when the various visitors leave, when the family retires to its own quarters across from mine, and when I fan myself to sleep under the air-stifling mosquito net.

It's the culture, stupid!

Sunday, June 26

WE ARE BACK in Tubaniso for three nights of debriefing. I have brought along all my possessions, hoping that I will be moved to some more comfortable quarters.

* * *

Ahhhh, long live cultural differences! As far as comfort, space, privacy or literacy of hosts are concerned, most of my younger colleagues appear to be better off than I am. One even has a sit-down toilet! In the U.S., most people would put an older guest into the most comfortable quarters available. However, the Peace Corps' Malian staff, put me with the "son" of the village chief who serves as liaison between the villagers and the Peace Corps. In other words, as a sign of respect for my age, I was put at the center of village power rather than of village comfort—perfectly logical, if you happen to be Malian....

Talking to the program manager for the Education Sector, I am slowly starting to understand why it is difficult for the Peace Corps to move me to a different compound. My host would lose face if I were removed from his compound and placed with another family, since everyone in the village would assume that I was unhappy with the family. Possibly this could also have negative effects on future groups of trainees who might no longer be welcomed.

I admit that my adjustment problems are clearly my own. The village host families try to do what they are told by the Peace Corps, though I doubt that they are given and understand the reasons for Peace Corps directives as to how we are to be treated. My illiterate 22-year old host "mother" simply does not know any better. How can you miss diversity in your diet if you have never experienced it? How can you be expected to wash your hands with soap, if you did not have the encouragement to do so as a child, if you have no running water, and if soap costs money you need to buy food? Furthermore, some villagers believe that using soap is unhealthy—which it probably is, if you use the home-made, lye-laden stuff available in the market on your face.

I decide that I will accept my fate for the remaining four weeks. If the majority of the Malian population can survive like this, so can I.

During our remaining stay with village host families we'll spend several days in Tubaniso. And next week we'll leave for a five-day visit to the actual sites where we will be working for the next two years.

Adjustment

June 29

I HAVE RETURNED to Kobalakoro where I am warmly welcomed back by the family. I brought back all of my belongings and I dig out of my suitcase an Uno card game. The children and some visiting adults have a great time practicing numbers and colors in Bambara, French and English. There is general consensus on what the numbers should be in each language. But agreement differs on the Bambara equivalent for *rouge*/red, *bleu*/blue, *jaune*/yellow, etc. I have to ask Mohamed why there seem to be several different words in Bambara for these colors.

* * *

I am still having problems dealing with the sanitary conditions of my compound. I come from the country that invented the fly screen, anti-bacterial soap, deodorant, Lysol spray, Listerine (actually a British invention), paper towels, Kleenex, etc., and where every seven minutes a TV ad tries to sell you some potion that either cleans, medicates or makes you smell better. And now I got transplanted to a Malian village!

Here flies swarm around the common eating bowl; people share without hesitation the few eating and drinking utensils that are available; instead of using toilet paper (considered dirty by many Malians) the villagers clean themselves using their left hand and water from a plastic tea kettle that is shared by the entire family, as well as by the frequent visitors to the compound (some just stop by to use the *njegen!*); people do not hesitate to spit into their (and your) immediate vicinity; chickens drink from the same water cup as the children; children relieve themselves in front of rather than in the *njegen*; sitting on the ground (even if on a mat) littered with chicken shit and other animal droppings does not interfere with one's appetite; and each meal appears to be seasoned with some grains of sand that originally surrounded the cooking pots.

I am convinced that our American concern and pre-occupation with cleanliness and sanitation has reached pathological dimensions, and that in the long run, this cleanliness cult will weaken our systems by making us less resistant to dangerous microbes. But hygiene and sanitation in a Malian village will have a ways to go before the villagers can enjoy similar life expectancies than their "western" friends.

Peace Corps 1963 vs. Peace Corps 2011

July 1

I HAD EXPECTED (and probably so did Peace Corps) that my previous experience of living in West Africa would facilitate my adjustment to Mali. I was wrong! How could I have envisioned that living conditions in a Malian village in 2011 would be worse than living conditions at an Anglican mission school for boys in Nigeria fifty years earlier? Then, I also lacked electricity and running water. There was not even a village well, and the necessary water supply was delivered daily by school boys from a shistosomiasis-infected stream nearby. But Mr. Anyam, the school's principal, had studied in England and was familiar with the basic amenities of western life. He made sure that we had a comfortable and clean place to eat, sleep, and work. Also, plastic garbage and dilapidated cars and motorcycles probably did only one tenth of the damage to the environment then than they do now. In addition, the influence of the colonizers—be they British or French—and the urge or willingness to imitate their example appear to have been much stronger right after independence than it is now.

Culture shock in retrospect

July 3

TODAY IS THE first day that I went exploring by myself. I walked to some interesting rock formations near the village. I think I finally have honed my survival skills sufficiently to make it through training. It took me a whole month! The Peace Corps Handbook lists 16 potential symptoms of culture shock. In retrospect, I suffered from seven of the 16 symptoms listed:

- Pre-occupation with health (in my case, actual symptoms of illness)

- Sleep disorder (in my case, due mostly to heat, noise, and lack of privacy)

- Feeling powerless (due to having lost all personal autonomy because of the imposed, highly structured family life and Peace Corps regulations)

- Anger, irritability, resentment (in my case, mostly directed at Peace Corps)

- Unable to solve simple problems (e.g., related to memory and language learning or just the inability to develop a system to deal with the *njegen*)

- Developing stereotypes about the culture (In my lucid moments, I am sure that my village experience cannot be generalized to all of Mali and Malians, but I catch myself more and more generalizing to all Malians rather than to the inhabitants of Kobalakoro.)

- Longing for family and friends (Godawful and spotty cell phone and very infrequent internet connection do not help!)

In addition I suffered from two symptoms not on the list of symptoms of culture shock listed in the Peace Corps Handbook: a tremendous case of lethargy, and not giving a damn anymore about my appearance.

Formerly known for my adventurous spirit, and as someone who in past travels barely touched ground before starting to explore my new neighborhood in concentric circles, I gave in to total lethargy and let the Peace Corps and host family make all arrangements for my survival. I believe that the paternalistic practices of the Peace Corps were part of my problem. This pre-service training must be similar to basic training in the military! We are shepherded around like children (which, admittedly, some of my colleagues still are) and lose all decision-making power over our own lives. If I had had to take care of my own needs, I am sure that I would not have succumbed to culture shock to the extent that I did.

Talking of my young colleagues: During my first stay at Tubaniso, one of the older volunteers who had already served some time in Mali told me that his major problems were not due to the Malians, but rather to the young, immature American volunteers. I am starting to understand his frustrations. American parents have raised a loud, self-centered, and self-indulgent offspring. I realize that some of the foul language (every sentence seems to include at least one "fuck"), inappropriate behavior, and need to band together is due to dealing with the stress of living in an alien environment. But sometimes I am embarrassed for my young colleagues because of their apparent lack of respect for our instructors, their loudness, and expectation that everybody just looooove American pop culture. Individually—one on one—all of my young colleagues are lovely, bright individuals, but as a group they leave something to be desired.

* * *

Another major rain storm. I thought that Boubakar had fixed the roof. But for the third time my roof leaks and I sleep on a wet mattress.

Fourth of July

THIS MORNING I picked up my first Malian outfit which I had made by one of the village tailors. To have a wrapper and blouse custom tailored cost 1,500 CFA or the equivalent of $3.00. There are some advantages to life in a Malian village—along with the huge, juicy mangoes sold in the market!

After language instruction (starting late because of

rain) we are transported to Tubaniso for an evening of July 4 activities. The group wanted to spend the 4th at the American Club in Bamako, but we are told that the facilities are oversubscribed by other Americans and there is no room for us.

I suspect that the Peace Corps does not want its representatives to carouse with the contingent of U.S. Marines who have arrived in Mali to help train the Malian military fight Al Qaeda. It is probably a wise decision not to encourage my young nubile colleagues to consort with a bunch of horny soldiers far away from home—quite apart from protecting the Peace Corps image from being "soiled" by associations with the military, CIA or other segment of the U.S. population that may not have intercultural understanding as its primary objective....

We'll spend the night in our huts in Tubaniso and drive back to the village early the next day for a discussion with Malian teachers regarding educational challenges. From the little insight I have gained already, these challenges appear almost overwhelming: primary school classrooms with over 100 students, insufficient and insufficiently trained teachers, few materials, and many parents who do not yet see the value of education—particularly for their daughters.

Reading, writing, 'rithmetic

July 5

WE LEFT TUBANISO at 7:30 a.m. and were directly driven to a primary school compound in Dialakorobougou to meet with a panel of ten Malian school teachers and administrators. The topic for discussion was "Challenges Faced in Malian Primary Education."

Primary education in Mali is not compulsory and there is no uniform system of teacher preparation. The preparation of the teachers who are present ranges from junior high (i.e., nine years of schooling) plus 45 days of pedagogical training to four-year university degrees with three to six months of pedagogical training at a teacher training institute.

Here is the list of challenges to education mentioned by the teachers:

- "Decentralization" of education: The national government's policy to decentralize education, which requires that the local communities become involved in educational decision making—while good in theory—is not functioning in practice. The government still dictates the national curriculum and the method of evaluation. What is left to the local communities is to try to come up with the financing of the schools.

- Changing governmental rules and expectations: Government programs and policies in the area of education are inconsistent and frequently changing.

- The new bilingual language education policy: In the past, all schooling was supposed to be in French, beginning in the first grade. The new language policy dictates that the first grade (and initial literacy development) be taught in the dominant language of the local community (in our case, Bambara); second grade starts French instruction; third grade increases French instruction; up to the sixth grade, when instruction begins to be exclusively in French for those who are able to continue schooling beyond the 6th grade. Again, the theory is sound, but the practice becomes problematic for a number of reasons: 1) Most African tribal languages are only emerging as written languages and there is a lack of appropriate instructional material. 2) Even educated Malians have some problems reading in their native language, partially for lack of practice, and partially because many languages still lack a uniform writing system. 3) Few Malian communities are monolingual, i.e., the various tribal groups and their languages are represented in most towns and villages.

• Language fluency of teachers: Some teachers have to teach using a language in which they are not fluent. This is true for the local language as well as for French, the linguistic legacy remaining from the former colonizer. One Songhai teacher complained that she was expected to teach in Bambara which was not her mother tongue. Of course, French—which is the national language of Mali used for administrative purposes—is not the mother tongue of any Malian....

• Low pay: Because of low teacher salaries, teachers

(especially men) often have to hold down two jobs to feed their families.

- Irregular pay: Teachers often do not receive their salaries on time. This is even true at the national university where teachers—apparently quite regularly—go on strike for non-payment of salary.

- Class size: A student-teacher ratio of 100+ students per primary class is apparently not rare.

- Double scheduling: Because of class size, teachers have to teach one group of students in the mornings and another group in the afternoons.

- Lack of materials: One teacher, for instance, reported having five books for 60 students!

- Lack of sufficient classroom space.

- Insufficient number of trained teachers.

- No respect for teachers and lack of discipline: One panel member attributed this lack to the fact that physical punishment was no longer officially condoned.

- Lack of appropriate school facilities: Often there are no fences surrounding school compounds, permitting animals and "undesirables" to interfere with teaching and learning.

- Lack of inservice training for teachers: There is no requirement for teachers to up-date pedagogical skills over time.

Several of us leave the session with a sense of hopelessness.

* * *

Back to Kobalakoro. Another rainstorm. The roof still leaks, in spite of Boubakar's claim that it has been repaired.

The meaning of statistics

July 6

DURING THE NIGHT I had to move my bed and suitcases because of a major leak directly over the bed. Since the mosquito net did not cover the bed's new location, the rest of the night was pure misery!

The children and Boubakar come in the morning with rags to wipe up the water from the floor. I want to call Peace Corps to fix the roof, but Boubakar swears up and down that the roof will be fixed. In the afternoon, during a light rain, several panels of tin roof are replaced, leaving the room and my belongings in a filthy mess. But I can no longer see light through small holes in the roof. Maybe, it finally works?

* * *

I am not sure how far one gets in Mali with using statistics to argue in favor of change or against some of the traditional practices that impede health or gender and social as well as economic development in general.

Personal or anecdotal evidence is the only "truth" that counts here! Let's take the example of female genital mutilation (FGM)—to which over 90% of Malian females are subjected.

The practice is neither prescribed by the Koran nor by the Bible. Clearly, it takes the cooperation and consent of adult females in the villages and in the families to continue that practice. It is female traditional practitioners who perform the procedure (it is illegal for MD's to perform the procedure in hospitals), and it is the mothers who agree to have it performed on their daughters either shortly after birth or at puberty before marriage, similar to male circumcision. The most frequently given reason for the painful, unsafe, unnecessary, and unhealthy practice is that without female excision (FGM), females will be promiscuous and not true to their husbands. . . .

The women who are arguing for the continuance of FGM obviously have survived it. So, what can possibly be wrong with the centuries-old practice? These survivors have had children without encountering major problems. Whatever after-effects they experience they don't know any different. If these women do not derive pleasure from intercourse they don't know any differently either. If you try to argue against the practice with statistical data, e.g., the rate of infections or death caused by FGM, difficulties during birth or permanent incontinence (caused by the most severe form of the practice—Type III FGM or infibulation, where the clitoris is removed completely and the cervix actually sewn shut), the statistical argument is meaningless to most village women.

Peace Corps impact on village life— a missed opportunity?

Theoretically, having Peace Corps trainees at village home-stays for two to three months could or should have a positive impact on sanitation practices of the families that host trainees. It is my understanding that these host families receive the equivalent of $6 per day for our food and lodging—a major economic incentive for people whose expectation for daily minimum wage is at most $2—$3. I also understand that the Peace Corps provides the families with training as to basic hygiene, sanitation, diet and food preparation before placing trainees. I wonder, however, whether the families are given the reasons behind the recommended hygienic and dietary practices. If the rationale is explained, it has not sunk in at my host family's place. For instance, the relationship between human (or animal) excrement or other bodily fluids and potential illnesses are clearly not yet understood. Some examples:

1) The Peace Corps wants the *njegens* to be covered when not in use to prevent flies from using the toilet holes as breeding grounds and carrying filth to food. To meet that requirement, my family puts a tin plate on top of the hole over the foot rests, about ten inches above the actual hole. Flies, roaches, etc. have no problem getting in and out of

the hole. Furthermore, it is absolutely gross to lift and replace the tin plate!

2) Peace Corps recommends that the family's drinking water supply—usually kept in a large earthenware pot in the compound—is covered to prevent animals from using it. The water pot in my compound is usually covered by a large tin plate. However, most of the time, the plastic cup that rests on top of the plate—and which is shared by all family members as well as guests to the compound—is left standing upright, and chickens, flies, etc. use it freely.

3) The dirty dishes are left on the ground for hours and become a major attraction for flies, chickens, roaches, etc. In the morning (when breakfast dishes and the dishes from last night's dinner are washed), Awa, the 12-year-old "daughter" (i.e., niece) who lives with the family and serves as Aissata's helper, utilizes a two-part procedure of using a bucket with (incredibly filthy) soapy water as well as a bucket with (initially) clear water for the job; for the rest of the day there is one filthy pot where dishes are washed without rinsing, and food is put right on top of the wet plate. After my complaint to Peace Corps staff about this practice, Aissata—when she remembers—comes into my little room and rinses the plate with water from my water filter before putting food onto the plate.

4) While Peace Corps encourages soak pits for waste

water to permit the water to soak into the often non-porous clay or laterite soil, my host family simply has dug a hole behind the *njegen* wall—not more than twenty yards from a village water pump—where the filthy, garbage-laden water stands as a breeding ground for whatever water-borne diseases there are.

5) If the reasons for using soap for hand washing have been explained to our hosts, the practice has not become routine in my family. The most unsanitary practice in all of Mali must be the use of the *selidaga* (plastic tea kettle filled with water) instead of using toilet paper followed by hand washing with soap and water. The same *selidaga* is used to clean yourself after toilet use, to wash your hands, to wash your face, rinse your mouth, drink or perform pre-prayer ablutions by the entire family as well as by visitors to the compound. I would love to have a bacterial test done on one of these things. . . . I am letting my soap lie around the *njegen* and happily observe that the bar is getting smaller.

I will recommend that experienced Peace Corps volunteers, fluent in Bambara, be involved in training the host families not just once but on multiple occasions, and that this training is used as actual project opportunity for us. If I ever get fluent enough in Bambara, I will come back to Kobalakoro to explain to my hosts and the neighbors the reasons for my insistence on what must be to them absurd—and occasionally even impolite—practices.

When Boubakar observed that some of my younger colleagues were having more health problems than I did, I pointed out to him that this was probably due to the fact that I frequently washed my hands with soap, drank only filtered water, did not use any ice, either chlorinated or peeled any fresh produce, etc. It could, of course, also be due to the fact that I grew up in Germany during the hardships caused by World War Two and previously spent two years in West Africa and may, therefore, be immune to some of the microbes that bug my younger colleagues raised with Lysol and sanitary wipes.

Preparation for life at our work-sites

July 7

IN THE MORNING we have language instruction. In the afternoon it's back to Tubaniso to receive our site assignment for the next two years. There is major excitement among my young colleagues. Apparently, everyone is fairly happy with their assignment—the large majority in small villages or small towns. I had been the only one who had an inkling of where I would be placed and am, of course, elated to have my site confirmed. I am also the only one in our group to be placed in the capital city of Mali, allowed to live independently (i.e., not within or near the confines of a family compound for security reasons) with relatively modern conveniences. I can barely believe it! In one month I will be able to close my door and not be the entertainment for the village population!

Tomorrow and Saturday we will meet with our Malian

counterparts who have been invited to come to Tubaniso to familiarize us with our sites, communities and jobs. I can't wait to see my new abode and meet my local counterpart, i.e., the assistant director of the art institute, a Mr. Bagayogo.

July 8

Most of the homologues (Malian counterparts and helpers/mentors of volunteers) arrived today for three days of joint training. Since I have a formal teaching position at a university-level institution in the capital city and am not living in a village or small town as the others, I don't have a homologue as such. Supposedly the assistant director at the art institute is my consultant or helper if and when I encounter difficulties. But I am told he is not coming to the training session. Instead, Jeremy, the volunteer I am to replace, came again from Bamako for the morning and I got some more insights into my future work assignment.

My colleagues' homologues are all male, except one, ranging in age from their 20s to 60s (age is hard to tell with older Malians). Some speak a little French, many don't. Some are literate. Some have worked with volunteers before. Some eat western style with a fork or spoon, others use their hand, but all enjoy the food and pile their plates high. The dress is mixed: Some are in western attire, some traditional. The two homologues from Dogon Country look "exotic" with their green turbans. One of them wears striking Tuareg jewelry.

I hugely admire my young colleagues who attempt

to communicate using their still very limited Bambara. I go through the lengthy greeting routines with whomever greets me, but I am soooo glad that I don't have to participate but can just observe.

July 9

Saturday morning all trainees take an hour-long written test to check whether we have internalized some of the information we are inundated with related to health practices, food security, personal security issues, and working in the Malian education or water/sanitation sector, depending on our assignment. The rest of the day we have joint training with homologues, conducted in Bambara with English translations provided by Malian Peace Corps staff. Very tiring!

July 10

The third day of joint training we are driven by van in small groups to various villages to practice PACA (Participatory Analysis for Community Action) methods for conducting an exploratory needs analysis for a community. About seven of us, accompanied by homologues and Peace Corps staff land in Baguineda Village to meet with the members of a Women's Cooperative engaged in composting and selling their product. Since I am the oldest, I get to accompany staff to the *dugutigi's* (village chief's) house for the official greeting, but he is not in his compound.

About a dozen women and several men are assembled in the classroom-like structure that serves as the cooperative's headquarters. A few of the women are here with small children. The women—as is customary here—are dressed in gorgeous traditional attire. Each outfit is tailored differently. I wonder where the money comes from to buy these lovely fabrics they are wearing. When I try to hold one of the babies present, the kid starts screaming with fear. The mother whips out her breast to pacify the poor little creature. I hope my white skin has not traumatized the child for life.

The group is divided into two: women and men. The actual practice session with PACA is slow and disorganized, but fascinating to watch. Many of the participating women are illiterate, and even those who are literate (with probably no more than a 6th grade education) have problems writing on the black board (literally a black board!). The writing becomes successively smaller with each crooked line. After a while, the process becomes painful to observe. There must be a more efficient way to facilitate community action.

Volunteers attempt to participate to the extent their fluency in Bambara permits, but most work is done by the homologues and Peace Corps staff. I am totally lost as to what is happening and believe my young colleagues are not doing any better. I send another silent prayer to Allah, thanking him that I won't have to use the PACA process at my work site to explore local development priorities, as perceived by Malian villagers.

We are told that our planned PACA meeting time has been reduced to half-day only, since someone in the village died and villagers want to participate in the funeral. The rice and sauce, delivered by Peace Corps vehicle from

Tubaniso for lunch, arrive late and are barely enough for all people present.

I have to use one of the local *njegens*. Dear merciful Allah! I thought the *njegen* at my host family site was gross! Here you can see the worms squirming in the fermenting mass below you in the hole. . . . I remind myself that one should not equate "civilization" with sanitation. I remind myself that Malians have a very rich culture that may in some respects even be superior to my own. For instance, when considering their family cohesiveness, their hospitality and generosity, and the willingness of those Malians able to leave their homeland to send home what amounts to the largest sources of foreign currency reaching the country. But it is difficult to keep that positive perspective in mind when one crouches over a Malian toilet hole surrounded by filth.

Before leaving the village, our group stops at the bereaved family's compound to express our condolences in the form of blessings which we quickly memorize in the van with Alassane's (our language and culture facilitator's) guidance.

I sit down on a steel folding chair which I thought was being offered to me among those assembled, not realizing that men and women sit separately: The men sit on chairs in the middle of the compound under a type of ramada; the women and children sit on mats on the floor right outside the house. Alassane, clearly upset by our cultural *faux pas* of trying to integrate the male circle, asks the female trainees to get up from their chairs and join the women. Ahhhhh, sweet memories of Nigeria, where

I was queen bee wherever I went, and where I could sit and talk with the men! There, as here, few village women speak the "official" language of the country (English in Nigeria and French in Mali), and it was and still is difficult to connect with my own gender.

A first taste of Bamako

July 12

AT 5 A.M. the first volunteers leave with their homologues to the sites where they will be living and working for the next two years. Some will be travelling for ten to twelve hours; some will have to take their bicycles along which will get them from where the bus stops on the main tarred road to their villages in the bush.

I am picked up at 8 a.m. by Peace Corps vehicle and driven to the art institute at the outskirts of Bamako. I initially expected that I would get introduced to the institution by Jeremy, but that plan had changed the night before. After some confusion as to who is to accompany me and introduce me to my new "employer," I end up with Founemakan—dressed in a dark, pin-striped suit, dress shirt, black tie, and very shiny shoes. Founemakan's regular job is to assist in training volunteers working in the area of small enterprise development. This is his first visit to the art institute as well as mine.

The institute's campus is located in the hills outside Bamako, right across the valley and in full view of the huge, official residential compound of Amadou Toumani Touré, the President of Mali, on the opposite hill. My first impression is a positive one: large, totally fenced-off terrain, interesting modern architecture, clean, well maintained grounds. Few people are around since July to October—the rainy season—is vacation time.

We find our way to the administration building. The assistant director, with whom I am supposed to meet is not yet in his office. We wait. After some time and negotiations in Bambara by Founemakan with people standing around in the reception area we are led into a small office—apparently that of the assistant to the assistant director whom I am to meet. He appears to have no idea who I am or why I am there, and we spend some awkward time trying to make conversation. I have difficulties understanding his French. We go back to the reception area and wait some more. The assistant director still has not arrived, but we are told we could see the director of the institution.

We are led into his office. He also appears to have no idea who I am, but after the initial awkwardness (every question I ask gets referred for an answer to the elusive assistant director), we are served tea and actually have an interesting conversation. I find out that the director is an internationally recognized artist who has exhibited in Europe as well as in the US.

Since Mr. Bagayogo, the assistant director, still has not shown up, we decide to leave the campus and to make an appointment for a future meeting. On the dirt road leading out of the campus grounds, we are stopped by the driver of a small truck, driven by none other than Mr. Bagayogo, who finally arrives two hours after what I thought was our scheduled appointment time. He walks over to my car window and apologizes profusely, claiming that he was taking his bath when the Peace Corps office called the evening before, and that he never confirmed the suggested meeting time. We agree that I should come back some time, accompanied by Jeremy, the volunteer I will be replacing,

I wonder whether anyone at the art institute was given a copy of my CV. I don't think it is very frequent that Peace Corps Volunteers hold a Ph.D. and have over thirty years of experience as teacher, teacher trainer and administrator. But extensive publication lists apparently don't count for much in my new appointment. While I certainly don't expect anyone to genuflect, I think the Peace Corps misses an opportunity by not publicizing the background and qualifications (not to mention the value in monetary terms!) of some of its older, experienced volunteers.

After this rather unsuccessful introduction to my new work place I am driven across town for quite some distance to my prospective place of residence, located in a part of Bamako called Guarantigibougou-Nerekoro. We stop at the large steel door of a totally enclosed, two-story, 12-unit apartment building on a muddy, pot-hole infested road, about 300 yards off the main drag in a "suburban" (West African style) neighborhood. Jeremy, whose position as well as residence I am to take over when he leaves in mid-August, is not home, but he has made arrangements for the security guard-cum-caretaker at the building to ready an unoccupied apartment for me for my four-day stay.

In comparison with my accommodations for the last six weeks, this is LUXURY—despite some broken windows, a loose-hanging faucet, and a leaking toilet without a seat. I get settled and wait for Jeremy.

When Jeremy arrives he takes me on a tour of the neighborhood, pointing out the *butigis* (tiny hole-in-the-wall shops where you can buy practically anything needed for survival), the nearest *boulangerie,* and tailor shops.

He greets and is greeted (in Bambara) by most people we encounter, indicating that he is a familiar face in the neighborhood. We stop at the neighborhood bar, "Svetlana," owned by a Russian, for a beer and buy a supply of the stuff to take back home. Jeremy tells me that many of the local bars double as whore houses, but "Svetlana" is the exception and I should not hesitate to come here alone. I am not so sure after a semi-clad female walks through the place on her way somewhere from a shower.

On the way back to the apartments we also pick up the ingredients for tonight's welcoming dinner which Jeremy has planned in order to introduce me to my prospective neighbors at the apartment complex.

My future neighbors are all Cuban artists with a university education who are sent by their government to teach for two to three years in Bamako. They range in age between their mid-thirties to their fifties. They receive a similar living allowance as Peace Corps Volunteers. However, their transportation and monthly stipend (equivalent to between $250–350) are paid by the Malian Ministry of Education rather than by the Cuban government. There is Lili who teaches dance; Irving teaches percussion (accompanied by a Cuban woman who teaches

Spanish at a local *lycée*, as well as the latter's teen age daughter); and Juan, who teaches painting. Another Cuban woman, Louisa, who resides at the apartments teaches flute but is not present. There is also a young American woman—a friend of Jeremy's—who has just terminated her Peace Corps service and will leave the country tomorrow.

The very tasty, home-cooked potluck consists of a Cuban soup, a Cuban-type pizza, an American potato soup, a Cuban bread-pudding-like desert and much beer. We avoid talking politics and have a great time. I will like it here!

July 13

Jeremy makes me aware that several of the apartments are empty and that I have a choice of which apartment to live in. I select an upstairs end unit, from which I can observe the enclosed courtyard below, as well as the street life with people sitting outside their houses and occasional small goat or cow herds passing by.

All the apartments are similar in size (I estimate about 400 sq ft) and layout: a living room, two small bedrooms, a bathroom with a miniature sink, a toilet, and a shower head over a drain in the middle of the floor. The standard furniture consists of a sofa, love seat, table and three chairs. There is also a large TV where one supposedly can access three stations. The kitchen is separate, next to but not directly connected to the rest of the apartment. The unit I have selected is slightly larger, has more privacy and better light than the others. I decide that I will move from my assigned to my newly chosen residence later today to get a feel for the place.

Jeremy takes me to explore the large, nearby Badalabougu market. We have a Coke at the Palais de Culture (a performance center for the arts), stop at a local ATM (thank God, it works!) and at a *tubab* store (Lebanese-owned supermarket where one can buy imported merchandise for exorbitant prices). We also visit the artisan market (fabulous!), the Peace Corps Transit House (where volunteers can spend the night when they come out of the bush to the big city for a couple of days), and have lunch at a small (and cheap) African restaurant near the Peace Corps office. Two of Jeremy's friends who are also completing Peace Corps service share our taxi when we drive back to Guarantigibougou. There will be another party at Jeremy's tonight.

When we get back to the apartments I start moving my few belongings upstairs to my chosen unit and start cleaning. I wonder whether I have made the right choice. There is only one thing that is more frustrating than not having modern conveniences, such as electricity, water, a toilet, etc. And that is having modern conveniences that don't work like they are supposed to. . . . Not only is my chosen apartment filthy (I am told that it was occupied by the Malian guards), it has a leaking toilet, a leaking sink, a floppy faucet, no shower head, non-functioning AC, a wobbly fan, no mosquito netting, loose electrical outlets, a stopped-up kitchen sink, a broken armoire, no curtains or curtain rods, etc. With the help of Daniel (the apartment complex' Christian caretaker-cum-security-guard) I

am going to work by raiding the other unoccupied apartments for what is missing in my own. Of course, I can't
do any of the repairs, but am hopeful that the art institute will have that done between now and when I actually
move in, after the formal swearing-in celebration that will
change my status from a Peace Corps Trainee to a Peace
Corps Volunteer on August 5.

* * *

At night we are surprised by a major rain storm. The
wind drives the rain through the loosely fitted living room
windows. What an incredible mess! All I have to wipe up
the water from the living room floor are some sheets. Oh
yes, and the ceiling above the living room starts leaking
and the fan starts making strange noises; so I turn it off
and continue the clean up job in the stifling, airless heat.
I want to go home!

July 14

I wake up feeling like a victim of the bubonic plague,
covered with mosquito bites. I guess I should have
moved the mosquito net from the downstairs unit. Since
the apartment windows are covered with fly screens, I
thought it was not necessary to use mosquito netting, but
the windows and doors do not fit tightly, and the buggers
get in anyway. Well, I guess I'll find out the effectiveness
of the malaria prophylactic medication (mefloquin) I am
taking weekly....

The water coming out of the shower and sink faucets
is awfully rusty, smells bad and tastes awful. There is, of

course, no hot water, but you don't really need it, except, maybe for hair washing. Jeremy tells me that his toilet already had to be replaced twice because of the rust. Almost all construction materials and plumbing parts come from China, are cheap and of low quality. There is apparently no quality control on what is imported into or used in the country.

Daniel helps me with the clean-up after last night's wet catastrophe. Assitan, the washer woman, comes by— her five-year-old daughter in tow—to pick up my dirty laundry. A man comes from the art institute to make an inventory of everything that needs to be repaired in my apartment. He promises a plumber and an electrician for tomorrow, but when I ask whether the water-stained ceiling and dirty walls can be repainted, he is non-committal.

Jeremy is occupied with his friends, so I am striking out on my own, with a visit to the nearby *boulangerie*. Among the few remains of seventy years of French colonial rule in Mali are fairly good French bread and pastry.

July 15

I savor my last full day in Bamako before having to return to the bush: No 5 a.m. awakening by the *muezzin*'s loud sing-song voice over the mosque's scratchy loudspeaker. Here in Bamako I have to strain to hear the calls to prayer from a mosque I can't see. No kitchen noises or smoke from the outside kitchen fire. No bleating donkey outside my door. No donkey manure pile or scratching chickens outside my door either. No one in front of my door with a water bucket. Barely a cock is crowing when I wake up at 6:30 a.m. And because of the whirling fan above my bed, I am not soaked in sweat. No masses of villagers passing by (and looking into) my window on the way to the water pump. I can get dressed without going into contortions to avoid being seen by the many visitors to the compound. No garbage strewn around the courtyard. I can't get away totally from plastic litter when looking out the bedroom window of the apartment, but I see a woman actually trying to sweep the unpaved street in front of a neighboring house.

I was able to make my nightly visits to the bathroom without groping for a flashlight, without having to get dressed, without having to wade through the muck outside (when it rains)—though here, too, I encounter a healthy-looking cockroach in the bathroom.

I can eat when and what I damn well please. No swatting at hordes of flies fighting over my plate. I still have to filter my drinking water, but I can keep it cold in a small refrigerator. And there is some beer in the refrigerator as well!

In my new place I have even surfaces on which to put my belongings. I don't have to search for medication or mascara that has rolled away on the rough, uneven cement floor as I have to in my village habitat. I can put my laptop and files on a table rather than on the garbage and chicken-shit-littered ground. I don't have to go to bed at 8:00 because there is no more light. The quiet during the night and early morning is delicious.

I am still the visible outsider, but most people in

Bamako have seen whites before and few children clamor to touch me or run after me crying "tubabu, tubabu" (white person, foreigner or Frenchman) in the streets.

There are no children or adults going through my garbage in search of anything useable—at least not while I am watching.

And there are no smelly, filthy, garbage-strewn pits holding the waste water coming out of local, open-air *njegens*. Mind you, for critical western eyes, there is still too much garbage, too much mud, too many potholes, too many flies and mosquitoes, too many rusted-out cars, too many non- or barely functioning pieces of technology—but compared with life in Kobalakoro or Tubaniso, this is paradise! I hope I can survive until August 5, when we come back to Bamako to be officially sworn in as Peace Corps Volunteers by the U.S. Ambassador to Mali. And I am raring to get to work!

In the afternoon I explore the area around the Peace Corps Transit House and discover the Bamako Radisson Hotel: an oasis of cleanliness with a mostly white clientele, and exorbitant prices. I treat myself to an ice cream sundae for the equivalent of US $12. I calculate that my monthly Peace Corps allowance will buy about 23 ice cream sundaes at the Radisson—not even one daily per month. . . . I also discover a beauty salon near the Radisson named "Black and White" and make an appointment for a pedicure and a hair cut for the following day, before my return to "the bush." Several Peace Corps old timers (i.e., those here for more than a year) have warned me that the haircuts they got in Mali were miserable, but I am starting to look like a bush baby and have no choice.

July 16

I pack up my belongings, reluctantly leave my (still mostly non-functioning) "luxury digs," take a taxi to the Peace Corps office to drop off my back-pack for the evening shuttle back to Tubaniso, and go to the Black and White Beauty Salon and Spa for my pedicure and haircut. The place could almost be in the States: clean, with somewhat dated décor. Everyone except me is black, and the luxury cars in front of the place provide evidence that the ladies, and one male customer getting a manicure in the place are not your run-of-the-mill Malians with an annual average income of $470.

Excellent pedicure! Shampoo with hot water—an absolute delight! And a pretty good haircut, although the male hairdresser does not follow my instructions. He is taking a long time to cut my hair and I wonder how many "white" haircuts he has done. I pay American prices, but it's worth it for an occasional treat. I find out that one can even get a massage at the Black and White. I may just blow my Peace Corps living allowance on one of those when I get down in the dumps.

Return to "the bush"

July 17–19

WE ARE ALL back in Tubaniso for debriefing. Publicly, my fellow trainees give enthusiastic reports of their future work sites—mostly in rural areas or small towns, mostly without electricity and running water, mostly living in traditional housing.

The Peace Corps requires that communities provide a two-room abode and a private *njegen* for its volunteers' exclusive use. So the majority of my colleagues will reside in two adjoining mud huts with their own toilet hole, surrounded by more or less privacy. Privately, some of my young colleagues admit to shock about their future living conditions.

I appear to have the most independence and creature comforts and am very grateful to the Peace Corps for my placement. I hate to admit it, but I am too old for adjusting to village life with stone-age living conditions.

July 20

We got back to our respective villages yesterday after our site visits and a debriefing in Tubaniso. Boubakar proudly shows me an electric pole that went up behind our concession during my absence. He has applied for electricity, but is uncertain when he'll get connected. In anticipation of the happy day, his sister, my name sake Salimata, has already given the family a refrigerator which at present serves as storage space.

It is incredibly hot and humid, but no rain. My misery continues with one additional feature: acrid smoke. Since the beginning of the rainy season, whenever Aissata believes there is a possibility of rain, she makes her cooking fire in a cubicle next to my room. Unfortunately, the smoke gets sucked right into my room and I sit there helplessly with tearing eyes.

After lunch (as always, rice and sauce), I sit outside my room and write in my journal. Little Hamidou (2 ½ years old) watches me for a while, then disappears into their house and returns with three colored pencils (two of them broken). I give him a piece of paper and he imitates my current activity by "writing" (i.e., scribbling) on the only flat surface available. Unfortunately, the surface of the weathered wooden bench is so rough that "writing" or drawing is practically impossible, and he soon quits.

Aissata also gets into the writing mode. She brings her literacy notebook (supplied by USAID) and shows me her homework assignment: basic arithmetic problems and copying words in Bambara. I help her with the arithmetic, using my fingers and numbers in French and Bambara: $8 - 2$; $6 + 3$. With numbers up to ten she has no difficulties. But when the problems get more abstract (e.g., $10 = 15 - x$), she is stumped. I am able to explain by writing down several examples, and she gets it. My 8-year-old grandson would beat her anytime!

For Aissata's writing practice I dictate some words in Bambara: *ba* (mother), *fa* (father), *Ameriki* (America). Aissata is delighted when I read back to her what she has written. We praise each other to high heaven for our intellectual achievements: her writing and my reading in Bambara.

But here is the problem: Adult literacy instruction in the villages is in Bambara, since few villagers speak

French. Theoretically, I agree with those experts in bilingual education who claim that it is easier to learn to write in your mother tongue than in a second language in which you are not yet fluent. But learning to read takes practice! Much practice!

How can one learn to read without having any appropriate reading materials? Advertisements and billboards along the road (Drink milk! Use condoms!) are mostly in French. Even at the National Museum all explanations are in French. There is very little reading material in local languages that is appropriate for children or adult reading practice. There is no *Dr. Seuss* in Bambara! I noticed that even literate Malians have problems reading in their mother tongue, since they lack practice, and there is not yet a standardized system of spelling.

During colonial and post-colonial times until quite recently, all formal schooling was to be (theoretically) in French. I feel conflicted about the recently introduced "experimental" primary school curriculum which starts with instruction in the local language of the majority group and slowly introduces French, beginning in second grade. By 7th grade, theoretically, all instruction is to be in French.

On one hand, the various ethnic and linguistic groups certainly have a right to their own language. If a language is not used, it dies (like hundreds of American Indian and Asian languages and dialects have died in the last hundred years). And with the dying language dies a part of a culture and much of local traditional knowledge.

On the other hand, research tells us that the younger

you start learning a language, the more exposure time you have and the more proficient you become. Further, unless a Malian is literate in French, he or she will be condemned forever to menial labor. There are no legal textbooks in Bambara (or Senoufo, or Malinke, or Tamashek, etc.); there are no medical journals in Bambara that report of the latest scientific developments; there are no engineering manuals, no ongoing written discussions on philosophy, history, the arts, etc. For that you need a language with a long tradition of writing, a long tradition of obligatory formal education, and a tradition of scientific, technical, and artistic openness and exploration. No African language, except possibly Arabic come to mind that meet these criteria. Though I also wonder whether Arabic meets the criteria of schooling and openness to scientific or artistic innovation.

I realize that the latter argument for an early start of literacy development in French also needs to consider the availability of trained teachers who are fluent in that language, and of the easy availability of age-appropriate instructional materials for all learners—two conditions that remain elusive in much of elementary education in Mali.

July 21

I was surprised to find my namesake (i.e., Boubakar's sister, Salimata) still in the compound when I returned from site visit. Supposedly she was to make the 12 to 15-hour bus trip back to her family in Gao before I returned from Bamako. I understand that she is staying longer because today there is to be a Diarra-clan get together to "sacrifice a cow." Apparently the animal sacrifice is intended to honor the ancestors, but I never fully understand what is happening and why. But here is the setting: In a neighboring compound (thank God the event is not taking place in the concession I live in) about two dozen women—colorfully dressed—mill about or sit on any available surface, laugh and talk. There are two huge cauldrons, one over a wooden fire, and one over a contraption connected to a bottle of gas. One cauldron contains the cow, cut into small pieces, bubbling in a rich broth; the other cauldron contains yellow rice, boiled with pieces of the cow's intestines for taste. There are also a couple of young men making tea, but no adult male is around.

Since in the village I am only known by my Malian name and, thus, am a member of the Diarra-clan as well, I get introduced to the women with the traditional (limp) hand shake. I ask whether I can take some photographs and they admire themselves on the little screen of my digital camera. None of the women except my namesake speaks any French. And even her French is very limited. One of the women asks me how many children I have. She looks to be in her thirties and tells me that she has nine! No one expresses it directly, but when I tell them that I have only one child—and that "only" a daughter— I am sure the women feel sorrow at my lack of fertility and inability to adequately fulfill my role handed down by Allah through the Prophet Mohammed: to breed for and be controlled by the males of the species. . . .

I claim to be a widow (which technically, according to catholic teachings, I am) rather than a divorcee, to avoid being branded as a loose or difficult woman. . . .

I hate myself for it, but I simply can't force myself to sit down with the women to eat from the communal bowl. I leave under some pretext and go back to my compound. There, I am joined by another Peace Corps trainee who is also named Diarra. She was introduced to her "relatives" after my departure from the site of celebration and she is as overwhelmed by the experience as I am. Eventually Aissata brings us a plate loaded with food and two spoons. Neither of us touches the pieces of intestines and other ingredients of undetermined origin in the rice. I am the only one who eats pieces of the sacrificed cow.

One party not being enough, there is also a wedding party under an open canopy constructed right next to the water pump in front of my window. People sit on metal chairs (one can rent them as well as other equipment for the frequent big gatherings which are popular here). The band consists of two males, playing tom toms of different sizes, three female musicians playing percussion on large bowls made of gourds turned upside down, and a female singer who loudly chants some monotonous-sounding (to western ears) melody.

Most of the women (again dressed to kill!) dance in circle formation. The few males present just sit. Apparently, everyone is waiting for food and for the newlyweds to arrive. I am invited to dance along with the women as well, but have to go to class.

When I get back in the evening, everyone has left and

only the stacks of metal chairs and the loads of garbage are proof of the gathering. Aissata and Salimata are still at the Diarra family gathering, but that too is breaking up by the time the muezzin announces sundown prayers.

Campement Kangaba

July 24

TOGETHER WITH SOME of my fellow trainees I am escaping the dirt and routines of Kobalakoro with an excursion to Campement Kangaba, a semi-developed "resort" located in the hills between Bamako and our various villages. Based on the glowing recommendations of an "old" Volunteer, some of my young colleagues had already visited the place on the first Sunday we were supposed to spend *en famille* and *en village*. Based on their enthusiastic descriptions, I decide to go along this time.

Getting to the place is on the complicated side. Several of my colleagues are taking their bikes. I, together with another trainee, decide on a combination of public transport in the form of an over-crowded mini-van (aka *sotrama)* and a taxi. Unfortunately, my travel companion and I find out that Sunday early morning is not a good time to get out of Kobalakoro by *sotrama*. We wait and wait by the side of the main road. No *sotrama*, but eventually a Mercedes stops, driven by a Malian man, who asks us in French where we want to go. He offers to take us part of the way.

Our chauffeur turns out to be an ex-diplomat who has served in Europe. When finding out that we are Americans, he gives a glowing report of his visit to New York where he spent a vacation. He also tells us that he bought an entire month' supply of meat in the villages, because meat is much cheaper there than in the city. He is now on his way back to Bamako. He drops us off in Dialakorobougou where we pick up three other trainees and continue the trip by *sotrama*. On the first try, we miss the turn-off sign to Campement Kangaba and almost end up in Bamako. We take a *sotrama* back and this time get off at the right place. We find a taxi that takes us the four kilometers into the "brousse" (bush).

And we arrive in paradise: a large, clean compound, crossed by decorative flag stone pathways, beautifully landscaped with tropical plants, an open-air bar/restaurant (with an extensive selection of wines), a wooden terrace with comfortable arm chairs, a pool area (with another bar), hammocks to snooze in, sleeping accommodations (traditional round thatched huts but with modern conveniences, as well as tent sites with access to showers and toilets), ball courts, horses, free wireless access etc. My young colleagues immediately head for the pool area. I sit on the terrace in front of the bar and—although it is only 10 a.m.—I have a beer and a *mousse au chocolat*. I also put in my order for lunch. I opt for an item rarely seen on a restaurant menu in a majority-Moslem country: pork chops (delicious!).

The owner of Kangaba is a Frenchman who has envisioned the place as a training site for local villagers. There is a large carpentry shop (beautifully made furniture and musical instruments), a tailoring *atelier*, a large garden. The gardener in charge proudly leads me through the various areas that grow the vegetables and herbs used in the restaurant. I see no weeds! There is a shop selling various hand-made traditional musical instruments, such as korahs, tom toms of all sizes, and xylophones; there is a boutique selling locally made weavings, clothing and jewelry. The only problem is that prices are not intended to be affordable on a Peace Corps living allowance.

Farewell to Kobalakoro

July 29

TODAY IS A very good day! The package that my daughter and grandchildren mailed almost a month ago has arrived. By chance, one of the "old" Volunteers who assists with our training had seen the package in Bamako, and after some prodding and several phone calls I get it delivered to Kobalakoro by Peace Corps van. I immediately start devouring the half-melted, chocolate-covered granola bars and dried cranberries, but then decide to start rationing them. My granddaughter made me two lovely bracelets which are admired by Peace Corps staff and trainees alike. My grandson thought that every grandmother in the bush could use a *Dr. Seuss* book. I also received some photos of the family. Alassane (our language and culture facilitator) who was born the same year as my daughter, greatly admires his "twin sister" in Florida and hopes to meet her in person when she comes to visit. In the meantime, I have to promise him that I give my daughter his regards whenever we are in contact.

In the evening we organize a thank-you and farewell dinner for our host families in the concession that serves as our instructional facility. I had suggested that we put on an American-style party (i.e., with plates, napkins, etc.), and serve something American to eat, but my young colleagues decide to take the easy road with Malian dishes (samé) and on serving the food Malian style in large communal bowls. We rent chairs and a huge cooking pot from the equivalent of a Malian party service for the approximately 35 guests expected. We do the shopping in the market but leave most of the actual cooking to the host mothers who have arrived at the concession early for that purpose.

Before starting to eat, we invite everyone to visit one of the two hand-washing stations which we have set up. A station consists of a bucket of clean water, refilled at the pump as needed, a bar of soap, and a large plastic cup to wet the hands and wash the soap off onto the ground and into the bushes. . . . A mess!

My special contribution to the feast are two packs of Foster Clark drink mixes which we mix with chlorinated water in the water filter. Awfully sweet stuff, but the people love it, particularly the many children who—by now—have invaded the concession from the surrounding neighborhood and patiently wait for their turn with the one drinking cup available.

Each of us has bought a farewell gift for our host family which we give to them privately: 10kg of sugar (particularly appreciated because of the imminent month of Ramadan where sugar-induced bursts of energy come in very handy), and ten small packages of green tea (used for the ceremonial Malian tea drinking tradition practiced mostly by males).

Some of us have added material for *a pagne* (wrapper) for the host mother who prepared the meals. This proved to be too expensive for those who are living in polygamous compounds, where several of the wives share the cooking duties.

I opt to give some money to Aissata, expressly for the children, although Alassane had advised against giving money. But in my opinion, Aissata has already an oversupply of *pagnes,* and the children, particularly the little girl, could well use some new underwear.

July 30

After final language tests in the morning we are free to go back to our host families to pack and get ready for tomorrow's departure from our on-site training villages. It starts to rain and continues non-stop until late evening. My room still has leaks along the walls, but thanks to Allah, the roof is tight.

A Peace Corps vehicle is supposed to pick up our bicycles and heavy luggage between 11:30 and 1 p.m. We have accumulated one hell of a lot of stuff by now: water filter, pails, a selidaga (plastic tea kettle to be used instead of toilet paper), kerosene lamp, mosquito net, blanket, pillow, straw broom, plastic fan, prayer mat and much, much reading material handed out during training.

The van shows up after 3 p.m. and the driver, Boubakar, and I slush trough the muck and flowing water, loading up my junk. For the rest of the afternoon I sit on a wobbly lawn chair (brought into my room by Boubakar), right by the door (the only source of sufficient light) and read. The family members escape the rain in their own quarters (which—by the way—I have never been invited to enter), and the concession is quiet, except for the periodic braying of the donkey and calls by the muezzin.

Because of the rain, Aissata delivers all my meals to my room—totally soaked by the rain. To eat, I sit on the floor and use the bench of my carpenter-made contraption as table. The rain has lowered the temperature and discourages the visits to the water pump. It is cool and quiet and I sleep well during my last night in the village.

July 31

I have survived what I consider the most difficult two months of my entire life! Today we are leaving our village host families and are going back to Tubaniso for four days of final preparation before swearing-in and moving to our work sites.

Lengthy farewells! One of the young Malian women who came to the school concession to see us off, presents me with a necklace made of pink plastic beads. I am touched. One of my young American colleagues even sheds tears at departure time. If everyone who asks for my phone number and promises to visit me in Bamako actually shows up, I will have full house! The scheduled 8 a.m. departure from Kobalakoro finally takes place after 9.

End of training

August 1–4

WE ARE BACK in Tubaniso, inundated with medical and security information, such as procedures relating to the Peace Corps emergency action plan in case we should need to be evacuated. Possible reasons for evacuation include Al Qaeda kidnappings, political unrest during next year's presidential election, epidemics—such as the growing cholera threat in the Mopti region, natural disaster, etc. We are assured that any such emergency evacuation is very unlikely. We also get to meet the U.S. Embassy's Chargé d'Affaires and have a tour of the Peace Corps headquarters with an introduction to the many Malian staff available to help us.

During the afternoon and evening before swearing in, the Peace Corps hosts a dinner for the trainees and members of our host families who are brought to Tubaniso by Peace Corps van. Since we are currently in the month of Ramadan—a time of traditional fasting for devout Moslems—we don't get any drink or food until after sun down. Unfortunately, the event is made less enjoyable by a heavy rain storm. The thatched roof of the outdoor area where we usually have classes and where we are all assembled starts to leak, and the entire group has to move inside the *refectoire* (dining hall) where one can't understand a damn word of any of the many speeches because of the thunder and the rain beating on the tin roof.

After our guests leave to be driven back to their

respective villages, my flip flops get stuck in the muck on my way back to our hut. I almost fall. Luckily, one of the young ones is close behind me and lets me hold on to her while I try to get my feet and flip flops out of the mud that is up to my ankles. This, too, shall pass!

Taking the "oath of office"

August 5

TODAY WE WILL be officially sworn in as Peace Corps Volunteers! All of us had colorful Malian-style attire made for the event by local tailors. We are decked out in our new Malian finery, trying to negotiate the muddy road to get from our huts to the dining hall from where the Peace Corps van is scheduled to leave at 8 a.m. I am one of two female volunteers who opts to wear a head scarf, not because I "want to go native," but because that is all I can do with my wet, freshly washed hair and without a mirror.

I have received permission to go directly to my apartment after the swearing-in ceremony. Since I am not coming back to Tubaniso with the rest of the group, all my belongings (bicycle, suitcases, back pack, medical kit, water filter, buckets, etc., etc.) are loaded onto the van together with twenty volunteers and staff. There is barely enough room for everybody.

We arrive at the U.S. Embassy, a huge, clean, well secured complex, surrounded by a high fence. Thank God, there are no soldiers standing around with machine guns and Rottweilers, like there were in Colombia when I worked there on a Fulbright grant. But security is tight with several check points, mostly staffed by Malians. Absolutely no cameras or phones are allowed!

We get shepherded into the inner sanctuary (after a second security check) and arrive in a long room, equipped with many folding chairs. There is, of course, Old Glory, and the walls are decorated with an extensive exhibit of photographs of Mali, apparently taken by young students for a photography competition.

The best part is the bathroom: the floor is cleaner than any floor I have encountered in Mali so far! One can sit (actual toilet seat that does not wiggle)! The flushing system works automatically! There is toilet paper! The sinks are clean and properly attached to the wall! The faucets appear to be screwed in correctly! And there is a mirror where—for the first time—I can see myself in the Malian outfit I had made for the event. Neither the tailor nor my village family or Tubaniso had a large mirror, and I had to go purely by "feel" when I tried on the two-piece outfit. I look good!

The actual swearing-in is conducted by the Chargé d'Affaires, since the Ambassador is on her terminating leave in the States, and the new Ambassador will not arrive until October. I have been asked to give the formal thank-you speech in French on behalf of our group. I had prepared it with the guidance of my language instructors, who—to my dismay—eliminated what I considered some of the best parts of what I had drafted and left me with a rather formal humorless statement:

Monsieur le Chargé d'Affaires des Etats-Unis d'Amérique, Monsieur le Directeur du Corps de la Paix, Messieurs les Ministres du Gouvernement de la République du Mali, Mesdames et Messieurs les Représentants du Corps Diplomatique, Messieurs les Maires, Chers collaborateurs, Mesdames et Messieurs du Corps de la Paix, Chers volontaires nouveaux et anciens,

Chers invités,

Bonjour!

Je suis Renate Schulz, professeur de linguistique appliquée, retraitée de la Université de Arizona. Je suis la volontaire la plus agée du Corps de la Paix au Mali. Je pourrais être la grande mère de tous mes collègues ici présents.

Je vais travailler dans le secteur de l'éducation ici à Bamako.

Au nom de tous les noveaux volontaires je voudrais remercier toutes les personnes qui ont aidé dans notre formation de base en langues et en culture.

Je voudrais remercier toutes les familles de Kobalakoro, Dialakorobougou, et de Baguineda Camp pour leur hospitalité généreuse et pour nous avoir permis de partager leur vie de tous les jours pendant deux mois. Ce merci va aussi aux boutiquiers, aux tailleurs, aux vendeuses de woson et de paté et à tous les membres de nos familles hôtes.

Il faut admettre que cette expérience de vivre au village n'était pas toujours facile. Moi, qui suis habituée à être indépendante, j'ai perdu presque

toute autonomie car—par respect—les Maliens fai-
saient tout pour moi. Il fallait vivre sans électricité,
ni d'autre commodités et être réveillée a 5 heures du
matin par l'appel du muezzin et le bruit des femmes
qui venaient chercher de l'eau à la pompe devant ma
fenêtre.

Au nom de tous mes collègues, je voudrais dire
un grand merci aux facilitateurs de langue et culture
pour leur patience et leur dévouement au travail.
Merci également aux formateurs techniques et de
cross-culture pour leur support sans faille. Que dire
de l'équipe médicale qui a su rassurer nos craintes? Je
n'oublie pas les chauffeurs, les membres de la cuisine et
tout le support-staff pour leur bon travail.

Enfin, merci beaucoup à l'équipe administrative
du Corps de la Paix pour la bonne organisation du
stage, pour avoir écouté nos désirs, trouvé des solutions
à nos problèmes et assuré la qualité de notre formation.

Mes jeunes collègues et moi, nous sommes très
contents d'être au Mali—dans une culture riche
et ancienne, un pays qui avait déjà une université
quand certains de nos ancêtres vivaient encore dans
les caves (je parle ici de la célèbre université de Tombouctou).

Nous sommes prêts à travailler avec les populations maliennes, main dans la main pour atteindre les
objectifs du Corps de la Paix qui sont:

- *Aider satisfaire les besoins des pays partenaires en personnel qualifié.*
- *Aider cultiver une meilleure compréhension des Américains par les populations des pays bénéficiares. Et*
- *Aider cultiver une meilleure compréhension des autres par les Américains.*

Vive l'amitié entre le Mali et les Etats Unis d'Amérique!
   Vive le Corps de la Paix!
   Merci pour avoir honoré de votre présence à cette cérémonie de notre prestation de serment.

My speech was followed by shorter versions delivered by other colleagues in Bambara, Malinke and Tamashek, the local languages taught in our group.

After the formal ceremony I am congratulated by Mr. Bagayogo the assistant director of the art institute, whom I am pleased to see among the many official Malian guests attending the ceremony. It appears that I will finally get to sit down with him during the coming week to discuss my assignment and his expectations.

I am interviewed in French by a young Malian reporter representing the local press and the Voice of America. He wants to know how I like life in Mali. I am afraid that the pause, searching for appropriate words, is more revealing than my actual answer. In an American context the expected response (sincere or insincere) would be, "I absolutely love it!" But I can't think of an immediate, unqualified answer. Obviously, Mali is a fascinating place to someone coming from Tucson, Arizona. So that is what I say. I wish someone had warned me in advance of the interview. I was not as articulate as I would like to have been.

After official group photographs we leave the embassy and are driven to the American Club. The driver drops off everyone and everything except the Education Program Coordinator, me, and my luggage. I am officially a member of the Peace Corps of the United States of America and am going to be driven to the place where I will rest my weary bones at the end of the day for the next two years.

The driver finds my apartment complex without difficulties and everyone present helps to unload my many pieces of luggage. Jeremy, unfortunately, is out of town on a final visit to Dogon Country before he leaves Mali next week. Daniel, the caretaker of the complex, has some problems finding the key to my unit. His many keys are unmarked and he tries them one by one. But finally he succeeds in opening the door. I notice that none of the repairs I had requested have been performed. My belongings are stored in the apartment and I and my "moving crew" leave to return to the American Club for lunch to celebrate with my young colleagues our induction into the Peace Corps.

On the way to the American Club we stop at the Direccion Regionale de la Police where the Education Program Coordinator—ever concerned about volunteer safety—wants to introduce me to the Chief of Police of the 11th Arrondissement where I will be living. Initially, no one quite knows what to do with us, but finally we are led to the office of the kindly older gentleman who serves as Contrôleur Général, Commissaire chargé du 11ième Arrondissement. When he finds out who I am and has gathered relevant information, he tells me that he will personally drive by to check on me. I tell him that I would very much like to see him again, but hope to have no problems. He and a female police officer lead us out of his office with many handshakes, farewells, and thank-yous.

* * *

My young colleagues are planning to continue celebrating their new status for the next 24 hours before returning to Tubaniso on Saturday, and on to their work sites on Monday. They will be spending the night at the Hotel Campagnard, preceded by dinner that will be followed by a late night visit to a night club. I opt to go "home" to unpack, start to clean, and settle in.

The author's host surrounded by his own and village children in front of the author's living quarters.

Author and her namesake, Salimata, in front of the author's room.

Salimata in the "kitchen."

The author's "host brother" in front of the compound's recycling system.

The famous njegen.

A village tailor.

Guests at a Malian wedding.

Preparing a wedding feast.

At the market in Kati.

Mali volunteers after the swearing-in ceremony. The Author is to the far right in the front row.

Musicians at the music "Festival sur le Niger" in Segou.

City transportation in Segou.

The author and participants at the English language competition.

Part III *Peace Corps Service*

Facts about the U.S. Peace Corps

History

Officially established: March 1, 1961

Americans who have served: 200,000+

Host countries served to date: 139

Although times have changed, the Peace Corps continues to promote peace and friendship by remaining true to its mission, established in 1961:

1. To help the people of interested countries in meeting their need for trained men and women.

2. To help promote a better understanding of Americans on the part of the peoples served.

3. To help promote a better understanding of other peoples on the part of Americans.

(from Peace Corps Fact Sheet 9/30/2011)

Getting oriented

August 10

I FINALLY GET to meet with Mr. Bagayogo, the assistant director of the art institute, my new boss. He sent a school van and two drivers to pick up Jeremy and me from the apartments and bring us to the institute. The trip took almost an hour.

The campus is still pretty empty because of vacation, but several of the administrators and department heads are working on site. He gives me my tentative teaching schedule (great! limited to three days a week, mornings only!), explains to me the grading procedures (Mali uses the 20-point French system which I still have not totally penetrated). He seems to be a very nice and competent man and I am looking forward to working with him. The only thing we have not yet fully resolved is my housing situation. We leave it with the decision that I will move from my present apartment into Jeremy's place when he leaves on Saturday. Mr. Bagayogo will then see to it that the leaking roof gets fixed, that the AC and bathroom repairs are done, and the unit is repainted—at which time I will move back. I am not holding my breath that this actually will happen.

* * *

After getting back to the apartment I note that the toilet in my current unit not only leaks—now it has also stopped flushing! Oh well, I keep a bucket filled with water next to the toilet. The water looks and smells incredibly rusty, and an oily film forms on top of the bucket. Good God, have I been showering with this??? Whenever there is a water outage (and they are frequent!), the water lines cough up a thick, rusty slime. I am almost envious of my colleagues in the bush who depend on bucket baths from the village well. If you have no other option, you don't get frustrated when you try the faucet and nothing happens....

* * *

I finally have learned to spell "diarrhea" correctly, because of my frequent need to use the word when consulting with the Peace Corps Medical Officer. Since yesterday I have the classic symptoms of giardia. It is kind of ironic that I get it now, when I am in control of what I eat, but according to the Peace Corps medical handbook, I could have caught the bug as much as a week ago, when I still was in Tubaniso.

Shopping Malian style

August 11

TODAY IT TOOK me four hours to buy a plastic table cloth. I also had a thermos bottle on my shopping list, but by the time I had found and bargained for the table cloth with aggressive shop keepers, I had no energy left.

Here is my day: I took a *sotrama* rather than a taxi to the main market. The transportation fare was great (1.75 CFA as compared to 2000 CFA by taxi). Comfort, however, was non-existent: 16 people plus their goods crammed unto benches surrounding the inside of a dilapidated mini-van. The trip took about an hour, since the *sotrama* stops whenever or wherever someone wants to get on or off. But even if it is neither fast nor comfortable, at least Bamako has a working, affordable public transportation system, which is more than I can say for Tucson, Arizona.

There is no question that one can get anything one needs in Bamako. The quality of the goods is, unfortunately, another matter, since China seems to sell in Mali everything rejected by the U.S. The entire city appears to be a market place with stands, *butigis* (small shops), ambulant traders, and stores all over. There is, however, no one-stop shopping. And I certainly hope there won't be any in the near future, since a Target or Walmart here would affect the livelihood of half the population who are all engaged in small commerce. There are no yellow pages (everyone has cell phones), and so far, I have not been able to determine whether there is a phone book for the capital city of this country. So, if you don't know where you can get what you need (such as a plastic table cloth), shopping is very time consuming.

I had barely climbed off the *sotrama* near the *Grande Mosquée* (the main mosque of Bamako) when a rasta-coiffed young man latched on to me trying to take me places and explain things. At first I resisted, but I could not get rid of him. After a while he was joined by another young man (I found out later that he was a jewelry maker from Mopti), so I traipsed around, led by Joseph and Jakuba.

The two of them called me *Maman* (Mom), protected my handbag (*Maman, faites attention, il y a des voleurs ici!*) and led me by the hand across the street through unbelievable traffic jams consisting of masses of people, *sotramas*, motor scooters, taxis and cars. Anyway, the 500 CFA (a little over a buck) that I gave Joseph after he hailed a taxi for me for the trip home, and the 4,000 CFA I paid for the necklace made by Jakuba were well spent! And on the way back home, the taxi driver proposed marriage to me, so all in all, it was a successful day.

August 12

I just realized that I have not had a hot meal since I got to my apartment. Jeremy sold me the dilapidated gas stove he used while here, but in the morning when I open my kitchen door, the place reeks of gas. The gas bottle is probably leaking or Daniel did not connect it correctly when the stove was moved. I resolve to light the stove this evening to boil some eggs (guinea fowl eggs—small, hard shelled, and dirty but delicious) and hope I won't blow myself up.

I am staying home, read and work on my journal most of the day, because the sky is grey and the clouds promise rain.

Reflections on Islam

MALI IS A majority-Moslem country with over 90% of the population adhering (in some fashion or other) to Islam. The country's constitution guarantees freedom of religion, and Malians appear to be quite tolerant of those with aberrant religious beliefs. Of course, everyone assumes that all of us *tubabs* (whites) are Christians, and I am not trying to abuse them of the contrary.

Malian Islam is definitely not the intolerant, humorless version of the Islam you encounter in Saudi Arabia or that is practiced by the Taliban. Very few women veil their faces; women are permitted to drive cars and motorcycles; music and dancing are part of everyday life; and the plastic arts are not limited to representing flowers and geometric patterns but use human or animal forms in religious as well as secular art forms.

Malian Moslems do, of course, practice the "five pillars of Islam" that every devout Moslem must adhere to:

1. Recite the Moslem profession of faith: "There is no God but Allah, and Muhammad is his messenger."

2. Perform ritual prayers five times daily after ritual washing. Prayer time is at dawn before sunrise, midday, late afternoon, just after sunset, and between sunset and midnight.

3. Pay alms to benefit the poor and needy.

4. Fast during daytime hours in the month of Ramadan (9th month of the lunar calendar).

5. Make a pilgrimage *(hajj)* to Mecca, if they are physically able and can afford it.

It goes without saying that instead of church steeples there are the minarets of the mosques here—almost as many as churches of various Christian denominations in the U.S. Even in Bamako you hear the five daily calls for prayer over the minarets' loudspeakers. (Thanks to Allah, my Bamako residence does not have the mosque next door as was the case during my stay in the village, and I can sleep past 4:30 a.m.). It also goes without saying that most Malian-owned grocery stores and restaurant menus do not feature pork products. But generally speaking, compared with such countries as Saudi Arabia or Afghanistan, I would call the Malian version of Islam "Islam Lite" -☺ And many people, particularly in the bush, appear to follow a strange mixture of Moslem and animist practices (such as the "sacrifice" to the ancestors celebration I witnessed in Kobalakoro). And superstitions are rampant! Who knew that albinos were a result of breaking the tabu against having sex during daytime hours????

Most Malians I come into contact with seem to follow the practice of fasting during Ramadan. This year, Ramadan is from August 1–31, and even during the rainy season daytime temperatures easily climb into the 90s. Whatever convinced the Prophet Mohammed to dictate to the believers that if you are healthy and no longer a child, if you are not pregnant or nursing a child, and if you are not travelling, you should neither eat nor drink anything between sun-up and sun-down for an entire month? Neither should you smoke or engage in sexual activities during those times!

Most of the world's major religions (e.g., Christianity, Judaism, Islam, Buddhism, Hinduism) advocate periods of fasting for meditation and religious enlightenment. While there may well be some medically sound reasons for occasional fasting, I know of no medical support for abstaining from the intake of fluids in the desert for practically all of the working day. In fact, the chief Peace Corps Medical Officer would probably go ballistic if you flaunted her recommendations to ingest at least three liters of water throughout the day! (Note: I found out later, however, that the Malian nurse on the medical staff is performing the Ramadan fast.)

Here are some consequences of Ramadan that I have observed: Life definitely slows down! My bank closes at 1 p.m. rather than at 3 p.m. While the little hole-in-the-wall grocery store across from my house still is open during business hours, I sometime have to wake up the shop keeper when I come to make a purchase in the afternoon. The bread is no longer fresh when I buy half my *baguette* in mid- morning, since everyone else apparently won't need any bread until evening. At the market, yesterday afternoon, quite a few shop keepers were snoozing at their stalls. If you can pretty much expect that workmen come late to an appointment, now they may not show up at all. . . . And Maimouna, the woman who does my laundry, complains daily of headaches, vertigo and weakness because she tries to do *karem* (fasting), although she is married to a Christian and tells me that she goes to church on Sundays. Go figure!

One problem with Islam, as practiced in Mali, is that

Allah is given responsibility for absolutely everything. Free will and self-determination apparently play only a minor role. It is not quite clear why the Creator has endowed humans with rational intelligence if they are not supposed to use it. Thus, students tell me, "I'll see you in class, *insha Allah!*" The ironing man bids me good bye with "Your clothes will be ready by evening, *insha Allah!*" The *butigi* owner informs me, "There may be tomatoes tomorrow, *insha Allah!*" And a bridal couple is admonished "May you have many children, *insha Allah!*"

If it is God who gives you children, who causes prices to rise, who sends pestilence, who provides a good harvest, etc., are you then absolved of the responsibility to plan your family, to watch the market, to fertilize your crops, to manage your environment and finances, etc.?

Another move

August 13

JEREMY OFFICIALLY TERMINATED his Peace Corps service yesterday and left this morning to start on his trip back to the States (overland via Guinea, Mauritania, Morocco and Spain—ahhhh, to be young again…).

I am moving into Jeremy's apartment, mainly because he had a wireless router installed there and it would probably take weeks to get that moved. Anyway, the place is smaller and has less light and privacy than the unit I abandoned. It reeks of cigarette smoke (Jeremy is a smoker, as quite a few of my young colleagues appear to have taken up that habit while here), and through the bedroom window occasionally wafts the aroma left by three large goats tethered directly below my window in the courtyard of the neighboring compound. The toilet in this place leaks as well, as does the kitchen sink; the electric outlets are loose, and the bathroom door only opens with force because of accumulated moisture. The door handle of the bathroom door is long gone. But glory be! the roof does not leak and the wind does not drive the rain through the windows as was the case in my former residence. Maimouna helps me with the cleaning and is ecstatic when I pay her 4,000 CFAs (about $8.00) for her three hours of work.

A Sunday outing

August 14

I DESPERATELY NEED groceries other than those available in the little *butigi* across the street that sells tea, sugar, cooking oil, tomato paste, soap, matches, sardines, bread, dry milk, flip flops, candles, cigarettes (by the piece) and soft drinks. So I decide to take the *sotrama* that passes one of the Lebanese-owned supermarkets and to bring my purchases home by taxi.

If you have to travel by *sotrama*, Sunday morning is the time to do so! Many of the little stores and stands are still closed, and at first I am the only passenger. But slowly the vehicle fills up and I am again crammed in like a sardine between all the other passengers. I do not yet know the route well and am trying to find a landmark where to get off. And suddenly I recognize Azar's—my destination. I yell "stop" and try to get up, but am held down by my neighbors who signal that what I am doing is dangerous. The *sotrama* slows down and finally stops and I get off among the reprimands of my fellow passengers. I am not sure what is being said, since everyone speaks only Bambara, but I express many *merci beaucoups* to those who saved me from a trip to a Malian hospital.

Near the supermarket I discover Amandine's, a Lebanese-owned *Boulangerie* and *Patisserie* that looks inviting with some tables and chairs arranged outside in the exhaust fumes. I treat myself to a *té au citron* and a huge, flaky, almond-covered *croissant*. Ahhh, what a luxurious life!

When I am half through with my supermarket shopping I realize that I will never have enough cash to pay for my purchases, and they don't take credit cards. I store my purchases with the cashier and find an ATM near-by. Thanks to Allah it works!

The living allowance provided by the Peace Corps is definitely not calculated based on the white-man's food available at Azar! Despite the so called "settling-in" supplement of 140,000 CFAs (about $300), provided by Peace Corps for one-time purchases to furnish our living quarters, I have had to raid my Tucson bank account on several occasions. Financially speaking, there are advantages to living in the bush where shopping is limited to the weekly market, and where they don't sell French brie, imported pears, and Beaujolais Village. . . .

The honeymoon is over

August 18

I HAVE ESTABLISHED an early morning routine to go up on the flat roof above the apartments to do some stretching exercises and enjoy the (still) cool breeze over the houses, construction sites and empty lots of my neighborhood. Like in other developing countries, mortgages to finance building projects are not very common, and people build only when they have acquired the funds to do so. Thus, there are plenty of half- or quarter-completed building projects in my neighborhood. Some never get beyond having a load of cement blocks delivered....

Usually I am the only living soul on the neighborhood roofs at this hour, but not today! On the roof of the adjoining compound is a man who gesticulates to get my attention and holds forth with a stream of Bambara that I do not understand. He points to the second floor and says something about "velo." I interpret this to mean that he has seen my bicycle, parked in a narrow space outside my living room windows, wants to know whether it is mine, or that he would like to borrow it. I make signs of non-comprehension, tell him in French that I don't understand and return to my apartment.

I don't know what causes me to check the outside parameters of my apartment after a while, but when I do, I note that my bicycle is missing. I become frantic, and go downstairs to report it to Daniel who is supposed to assume his duties after the night watchman leaves at 6 a.m. His door is open (as is the door to the courtyard) but he is sleeping deeply. I decide to call Peace Corps Security instead, since Daniel barely speaks French. When I come back out, a *boubou*-clad man has entered the courtyard, carrying his prayer beads. He is having a loud discussion with Daniel who has finally woken up. With broken French, the man explains to me that the neighbor man (the one who tried to communicate with me on the roof) was awakened about 4 this morning by a strange noise. He interrupted a thief as he tried to lift my bicycle over the wall. The thief fled, leaving the bicycle behind on the neighbor's side of the compound wall.

The *boubou*-dressed man accompanies me—still dressed in my night clothes—around the corner to the compound of the neighbor. And voilà, my bicycle! It is still locked with the chain I had fastened around the wheel and frame! I run back to my apartment to get the key for the bicycle lock, and at the *butigi* across the street buy ten packets of tea and two pounds of sugar (a traditional gift to show one's appreciation). I give half of my purchase to the "interpreter" and half to the neighbor. The "interpreter" makes clear to me, however, that the neighbor also expects a "gift" for the recovery of the bicycle. He suggests 1,000 CFAs which I gladly hand over.

I inspect the walls of the stairwell and the high wall that separates the apartments from the neighboring compound and am totally baffled as to how anyone (even two people) could have carried or lifted a bicycle across. Also, since I am on the second floor of a totally enclosed courtyard, who, except the caretaker or night guard (and their many visiting friends and family members), even knew that I had a bicycle?

Anyway, the feeling of security that I enjoyed up to now is gone. From now on, I will barricade myself behind locked doors, like the rest of the Malian population does.

I send the bike and its accoutrements (pump, helmet, repair kit) back with the Peace Corps Security Coordinator and resolve to do without that means of transportation. It was unlikely that I would use it anyway because of the conditions of the neighborhood streets. And furthermore, among the few bicyclists I saw in Bamako, I never saw a 71-year old woman ride one . . . .

* * *

One other puzzling experience—I don't know whether it is related to the bike theft or not: Shortly before the arrival of the Peace Corps Security Coordinator, Daniel and a French-speaking friend, Abdul, who appears to live with him periodically, come up to my apartment. If I understand correctly what Abdul is saying, Daniel wants me to keep the pay he is receiving as caretaker (30,000 CFA or about $60 per month) for safe keeping, since he fears it will be stolen in his place downstairs, and also, so that he does not fritter it away. Does this request have anything to do with Daniel's efforts to save face because of the theft of my bike? I show reluctance, they leave, and the matter stays unresolved. I hope he is not really planning to give me his money for safe-keeping!

The end of Ramadan

August 30, around 10:00 a.m.

TODAY, MALI CELEBRATES the end of Ramadan. Although the sky was totally covered by clouds in Bamako last night, apparently someone saw the signs of the beginning new lunar cycle that terminates Ramadan and reported it "to the commissioner" who is in charge to determine such things.

I am sitting on the narrow, second-floor terrace overlooking the street in front of the apartments. The little *butigi* across the street is open, its owner sitting in front, wearing a new lilac-colored *boubou* and turban. About half a dozen men—all dressed in new *boubous*—walk by. They wave to me and wish me "bonne fête" before entering the court yards across the streets for greetings.

Several groups of girls—also in new attire—stop at the door to the neighbors' compound as well. One carries her little brother or sister on her back. One nubile maiden is wearing silver-colored high heels, totally unsuitable for the wet, mud-hole-covered road. They sing-song a lengthy recitation in Bambara. I wish I understood the meaning.

A group of young boys pass by, also newly attired— but this time in western-style pants and shirts. One little one is wearing sun glasses up-side down over his ears!

The only people missing are adult women. I assume that, as always, if they are not out selling condiments (tiny bags of salt, pepper, garlic, oil, etc. bought by many families fresh every day) or the few fruits and vegetables available this time of year (the rainy season is not in vain called the "hungry season" in Bambara), they are at home minding the kitchen fires, cooking, pounding millet or rice, roasting peanuts, sweeping, doing laundry or taking care of small children, if there are no older siblings around to care for them.

I wish I could take a video of the fashions and colors passing by: New *bazin* (wax-covered cloth beaten to a glossy sheen), gorgeous patterns for the females, most often uni-colored for the males. Some of the girls are wearing outfits made of the identical fabric, apparently sisters. The girls not yet wearing head covers have freshly braided hair-dos, the tiny braids held by dozens of multi-colored bangles.

My apartment is located in one of the wealthier "suburbs," although the compounds are very mixed in size. Several cars and motorcycles empty loads of people at neighboring houses to share the celebrations. One of the motorcycles carries an entire family of five people.

Once people enter the compounds, there appears to be little mixing of genders. This reminds me of Thanksgiving in the 50s in rural Minnesota when the women congregated in the kitchen and the men in front of the TV.

Cholera

August 31

AN UPDATE ON the Malian cholera epidemic arrives by
e-mail from Peace Corps Bamako. As of August 23, there
are 882 confirmed cases of the disease. Quite frankly, I am
amazed that cholera is not more rampant during the rainy
season in Mali. I got caught by the rain in the Badalabougou market last week. The market place turned into
a filthy river: vegetable peelings, chicken feathers, animal
intestines and lots of undefinable gunk, including, I am
sure, the contents of some neighborhood *njegens*. . . . The
local newspapers carried a report about the dismally
unsanitary conditions in some of the open markets. Given
the state of public sanitation I wonder what can be done
to prevent such diseases.

The positive side of my wet market experience was
another encounter with Malian friendliness. One of the
vendors offered me his high, bar-stool-like seat under the
plastic tarp covering his market stall. There I sat—high
and (relatively) dry, while he stood in the flowing sludge.

September 2

I am going back to the Ministry's Language Center
to discuss some possible work there before the start of
the semester at the art institute—my regular job. They
ask me whether I could work with air traffic controllers
at the Bamako airport to give them additional English
practice to understand incoming pilots. Merciful Allah!!!!

What do pilots say at landing and take-off? Anyway, the Director of the Language Center will call me early next week with a possible assignment.

Life of the middle class

September 3

A HUGE RAIN storm during the night! I close all windows and go back to sleep. At day break I wake up, get out of bed, and almost slip in a puddle of water. Most of the apartment floor is covered with water. I inspect windows, door, ceiling, but cannot find the source of the leak. I wake up Daniel, the caretaker, and Henri, the night guard. They come both up to the apartment and appear to be as puzzled as I am about the inundation. I note that the extension cords and electric outlets are lying in water and am petrified that either someone will electrocute himself (I am not going to touch those plugs!) or my computer will no longer work. Daniel gets buckets and rags and cleans up the floors. After he leaves, I re-inspect the ceiling, floors, windows, door. I note wet spots along the baseboard of the inside wall, both in the living room and second bedroom. I finally figure out that the water must have come from the roof, where Daniel screwed around yesterday, trying to install a new TV cable for my still non-functioning TV. I again call Daniel and show him the wet areas on the walls.

Thanks to Allah, Mohamed comes around 9 a.m. to pick me up for Bambara lessons that are to be at his house today. I use him as interpreter to find out what the hell

Daniel is planning to do so my place won't get inundated again during the next rain. Daniel apparently has already figured out the problem and has cemented over the hole he created yesterday on the flat roof to install the cable that is still not working.

Mohamed and I drive in his old but well maintained Mercedes to his house in an urban neighborhood. Even the seat belts and windows of the car still work—which is more than I can say for most of the taxis here. . . .

Mohamed is monogamous, and although he is a devout Moslem, he and his wife must be familiar with principles of birth control, since they only have three children. Mohamed shares his two-story abode with his wife, two daughters (one working as a hydraulic engineer, and one still in training as a pediatrician), one son (studying pharmacy at the university), his "sister" (no blood relation), a boy of secondary school age (I never did find out his relationship to the family), and a young girl working as maid. The small courtyard and house are spotless. So, this is apparently how the Malan middle class lives.

We take off our shoes and sit in the small downstairs living room, furnished with an upholstered couch, love seat and arm chairs around a coffee table which seems to be standard living room furniture in Bamako. There is also a glass-doored china cabinet filled with knick knacks. The only wall decoration is a photo of Mohamed's wife on pilgrimage to Mecca. He, himself, has not yet been to Mecca but hopes to go next year, *insha Allah*!

For Bambara lessons we move upstairs to the second

floor to an airy terrace overlooking the street, between a second, larger living area, some bedrooms and a modern, western-style bathroom. However, there is a *selidaga* rather than toilet paper and I find no soap or towels. Mohamed apologizes for the lack of appropriate living-room furniture upstairs. He explains that he does not believe in going into debt, so they will wait until there is money available for additional furniture.

After language lesson I get to meet Mohamed's wife who was not at home when we arrived. She—like Mohamed—is in her early fifties (I estimate), works for the Ministry of Education and—glory be! speaks French. She excuses herself "to go wash up."

Mohamed's daughter sets the small table and brings the food, prepared in the courtyard below. Mohamed and I are eating alone. The food is delicious: French fries, fried plantains, fresh green beans with carrots, and a savory beef stew (first chewable beef I have had in this country!). We eat western style (i.e., from plates with cutlery), but I note that the women of the house eat from a common bowl in the court yard below. After I have pigged out with several helpings, Mohamed's daughter brings the second course: rice and sauce. I am too full to eat more and hope I am not being impolite by not even tasting the dishes. Mohamed also is not taking any of the rice. I don't know whether he is trying to be polite or whether he is as full as I am.

When I want to take leave after lunch, I have to wait awhile to say good bye to Mohamed's wife, because Mohamed tells me that she is praying. After several good-byes and thank-yous I insist on taking a taxi home, so

Mohamed and his family can finally start their week end. By the way, Mohamed is an excellent language instructor, providing clear grammatical explanations followed by immediate lengthy practice. I have to use him as my model when I start teaching myself.

How to scare small children

September 5

WHEN I WAS a child in Germany, we had a counting rhyme that started "Who is afraid of the black man?" (*Wer fürchtet sich vorm schwarzen Mann?*). I wonder whether children here use something similar to warn of white people. When I try to be friendly on the street, quite a number of toddlers start crying and seek protection with their mothers. I don't blame them. I must be a frightening sight: large green eyes, whitish skin with all blemishes clearly visible, and light hair that stands in all directions behind my hair band. I appear to be the only "tubab" (white person) in the huge area called Guarantigibougou—Nerekoro. At least I have not yet seen any other pale face on my walks. And even in central Bamako, the only whites I encounter are at the Peace Corps office, and at the very few restaurants and supermarkets frequented by expatriates.

As to the adults in my neighborhood, they sit and look at me with earnest faces until I smile, wave or greet them in Bambara. Then large smiles spread across their faces and they start with the lengthy greeting ritual to welcome me to the neighborhood: "How are you? And how is your family? And how are your children? And how is your country?" etc. The expected response is, of course, that everyone and everything is alright. Not as if I could explain in Bambara if anything were not o.k.

* * *

Today I had dealings with my washer woman/cum cleaning lady who came to dust, my ironing man who lives across the street (I don't own an iron), my personal tailor around the corner (I am having a blouse made since the tops I brought are slowly starting to disintegrate because of the rough laundry methods), and my personal carpenter who came to the house to take the measurements for a book case and to see whether anything can be done to circumvent the locks on the armoire which never open when I want them to. There was also Daniel who tried to re-adjust the TV—for the umpteenth time—even though I had hired an electrician yesterday to fix that, as well as the loose electrical outlets in my apartment. Ah, the life of luxury where I don't have to do a damn thing myself that resembles housework or maintenance!

Trip to Dogon Country

September 9

NEW PEACE CORPS Volunteers are not supposed to travel outside their region for the first three months at their working sites. But I have received special permission to travel, since I won't be able to explore the country once the semester starts in October and I have to work every day. So I am off to Dogon Country in the northeastern part of Mali.

Together with three "old-timer" volunteers returning to their stations from Bamako I am taking the Peace Corps shuttle to Sevaré—an eight-hour drive to deliver mail and medications to the regional headquarters—via pit stops at Peace Corps rest houses in Segou and San. Sevaré is located in the most northeastern part of the country that volunteers are permitted to travel to. The rest of the country is off-limits to us because of Al Qaeda activities in northern Mali.

The approximately 640 km from Bamako to Sevaré offer little in terms of variety of landscape: flat terrain, brush and grass land (lovely green at this time of year because of the rainy season), with the occasional tree. I wonder what the locals will do when the supply of firewood gets exhausted.

When my young travel companions find out that this is my second stint in the Peace Corps, they want to know what has changed in the past 46 years since I served in Nigeria. They are amazed when I tell them that we had no computers, no cell phones, no Skype; that the AIDS virus had not yet transmuted from apes to humans, and that there was no supply of condoms in the Peace Corps medical kit. There were no Peace Corps shuttles for a monthly trip out of the bush; there was no on-site training or village homestay; and generally, we had to be much more independent and self-sufficient in the 1960s than volunteers have to be now. My husband and I were dropped off with our suitcases by the Igbo driver, and that was the last we saw of any Peace Corps personnel or Peace Corps vehicles until we had figured out a way to get out of the bush weeks later. They are equally surprised to hear that some forty years ago in Nigeria, no Peace Corps Volunteer lived in mud huts, even though electricity and running water were as elusive there then as they are in many Malian villages today.

Before my departure to the Mopti region I had sent text messages to the three young men from my group who are stationed there to invite them for dinner in Sevaré, provided they could make it into town. I am delighted to find Emmanuel at the Sevaré rest house when I arrive. Matt could not make it, and Zach did not respond. I hope he is o.k., since he had all kinds of health problems during training, including a weight loss of over 25 pounds.

Emmanuel updates me on the latest news from our group. Of originally 24 trainees, 21 are left. The latest departure is the young woman who I predicted would not be able to adjust to conditions in the bush. And one young colleague had to return to the States on emergency leave to attend his sister's funeral. She had committed suicide. I hope he has the strength to come back.

September 10

I am delighted that Diallo, the Peace Corps driver, has to drive to Bandiagara today, the beginning of Dogon Country—my planned destination. Two "old timers" plus Emmanuel and I ride along. When we arrive at the Peace Corps resthouse in Bandiagara around nine a.m., I am finally able to reach by cell phone Amadou, the Dogon guide recommended by Jeremy. I had tried to call him multiple times the night before, but never got a connection since many areas in Dogon Country are off the cell phone grid. Amadou had come to Bandiagara, waiting for my call, and by 10 a.m. I am off to Sangha, a Dogon village on the plateau about 64 km from Bandiagara that serves as entry point for many visitors who come to explore the area. Because of the cost of the excursion Emmanuel decides to stay in Bandiagara.

I ride in an SUV with three young Malians, while Amadou follows on his *moto* (motor scooter) which had brought him from his home village early this morning.

A couple of miles outside Bandiagara the tarmac stops. The rocky, sandy trail can only be negotiated by four-wheel-drive vehicles or by *moto*. The landscape becomes interesting: large boulders on a huge, rocky plateau, little vegetation, an occasional Dogon settlement with the *banko* (mud) buildings and characteristic cone-shaped, thatch-covered *greniers* for grain storage. At times we are driving on bare rock—the trail no longer discernable. Twice we have to back up to let a truck pass.

Finally we arrive at Sangha. I will not even attempt to describe a Dogon village: We walk between the tightly packed mud houses on very narrow paths; we pass the menstruation house where women are banished during their monthly period; we admire the compound of the *hogon* (spiritual leader of animists) who—according to Amadou—"cannot be touched by anyone, and who—rather than wash himself—is cleaned with the tongue of the sacred snake who lives in the compound." Amadou does not let me touch the stone wall surrounding the *hogon*'s compound, because if one of the rocks gets dislodged, I have to sacrifice a sheep or goat! The village looks amazingly clean but very, very poor. Amadou tells me that all the people in the village have the last name of Dolo, and that the inhabitants of other Dogon villages also have an identical last name.

We have lunch at the small, charming Hotel/Campement Anougué. I am totally dehydrated and down three soft drinks. Amadou tells me that the hotel's owner has a wife in Poland whom he visits every year. He also assures me that this Polish wife does not mind that the owner also has a Malian wife and a child locally. I wonder whether the Polish lover knows that she is "married," and how Polish laws deal with polygamy.

Amadou and I begin the 6km or so hike to Ireli, a Dogon village at the bottom of the Bandiagara escarpment that has been recognized by UNESCO as a World Heritage Site. The first couple of kilometers we walk on pretty flat terrain across the rocky plateau. There is not really a path, but Amadou knows the way.

We pass a divination site, a rectangular area, divided into a number of separate small "fields" by rows of stones. Within each stone-encased field there are tiny squares, marked by lines drawn into the earth with a stick. And in each of these small squares are stuck between one and four short sticks. Amadou tells me that the sticks represent questions that have been posed by locals the day before. During the night "the fox" (I assume he really means hyenas), who is attracted by peanuts which are strewn around the area, comes to answer the questions. (I see dog-like tracks all over the divination area). However, only the local fetishist/ diviner can decipher the answer. Amadou asks me whether I want to ask a question. I decline, using as excuse that I would not be able to return to find out the answer.

And then begins the descent!!! Allah the All-Hearing and All-Seeing! Allah the Just and Benevolent! I don't think Amadou realizes that I am most likely older than his grandmother. I should have informed him of my age and physical condition before going on this trek. This is the Grand Canyon without a discernable paths and a drop of about 600 meters! In the rock wall above us are the cliff dwellings (very similar to those in Northern Arizona and Southern Colorado), formerly inhabited by the Telem, believed by the Dogon to have been a pygmy-like people "who could fly." The cliff dwellings are now used as burial caves by animist Dogon who deposit their dead there, hauled up into the cliffs with ropes.

After a couple of hours my knees start shaking and I am making more and more use of Amadou's strong arms to negotiate the rocks. To avoid tumbling into the crevices I slide down some areas on my *derrière*. I am petrified that we won't make the *campement* before nightfall. But we do!

It is getting dusk when the village at the bottom of the escarpment comes into sight. I am too exhausted to follow Amadou's explanations of what I am seeing. But I do note a jeep in the valley below and find out that for the equivalent of $100 plus gasoline I could have hired a four-wheel-drive vehicle to bring me here....This is almost like the German or Austrian Alps, where you subject yourself to an absolutely exhausting climb, only to arrive at a restaurant on top of the mountain, surrounded by buses in the parking lot. Well, not quite! This is definitely more rustic!

Arriving at the *Campement* "Emil Douyon" nestled against the escarpment, I can barely climb the steps up to the open roof which is surrounded by several window-less rooms, where a table is set for us. Rustic is an understatement! After a shower (in the dark, no towel), a large bottle of beer, and pasta with an oily sauce I come back to life.

The rest of the night is the most romantic night I have ever spent without a man! I am the only tourist in the *campement* and have an entire roof as my "bedroom." I lie on a two-inch foam mat under a mosquito net held up by tree branches precariously fastened to the side of the flat roof. Oh well, if the damn net collapses it won't kill me! There is a full moon above me and the shadows of the village huts crawl up the black cliffs of the escarpment. Occasionally, I hear the loud braying of a donkey (same godawful noise made by the donkey in Kobalakoro), the noises of a goat that can't sleep, and somewhere someone is playing a battery-operated radio. Amadou has his quarters above me on an adjoining roof. I am pleased to see that he also uses a mosquito net. Thanks to Allah the Merciful, I am so dehydrated I don't need to use the toilet during the night. Since I left my flashlight in Bamako, this would have been quite an adventure....

September 11

Today is the fateful day that—ten years ago—transformed America from the Land of the Brave to the Land of the Afraid. The Dogon people are still to a large extent animist, so I probably don't have to worry here about an Al Qaeda attack to celebrate 9/11.

The Dogon are no friends of Moslem extremists. Since several Al Qaeda kidnappings by AQIM (Al Qaeda in the Maghreb) in the north of Mali last spring, tourism to the area—apart from subsistence agriculture the main livelihood of the people—has practically died. Wherever Amadou takes me, I am the only tourist and the only white. What was a poor area to begin with is now destitute. I am spending what I have left on Malian currency (CFAs) on locally-made handicrafts that I need like a hole in the head (and that Amadou has to carry), just to give the people some income. All I have left with me on money now is my emergency stash of eighty U.S. dollars. Thanks to Allah, the only foreign currency they accept is Euros, or I would have spent that too.

* * *

Unfortunately, what comes down must go up! Around 7:30 a.m., after breakfast (dry French bread and Nescafe with powdered milk), we leave for the return journey to Sangha. The several kilometers between Ireli and Banani are on a flat, sandy path through millet fields. Then the 600-meter climb up the escarpment begins. Climbing up is easier than down, but equally exhausting. I am passed by women who look my age but are half my size, carrying huge loads on their heads, going to barter the little produce they can spare at the weekly market in Sangha (the Dogon week has five days).

I wonder whether our nutritional emphasis on eating proteins is oversold. These people barely get any protein, but they are certainly tougher than I am. Climbing up at about an 80-degree angle into the canyon on stairs hewn into the rocks, I ask Amadou how old or sick people get out of here. He answers that the old or sick stay at home. And the sick either get better or they die!

We get back to Sangha around 11:30 a.m. According to Amadou, we made the return trek in good time. We stop for lunch at the same place as the day before. Since lunch is not yet ready, a mat is put on the ground for me next to the tables under the ramada. I promptly fall asleep.

After lunch (pasta and stew) we pass by Amadou's compound where he introduces me to his father, sitting in the shade in front of his hut. The father's several wives are at the market selling things. Amadou translates for me to tell his father that I feel like Amadou's grandmother and that he can be very proud of his son. The old man (younger than I am!) laughs and shakes my hand.

The Sangha market is a chaotic beehive. People come here from all over Dogon Country. The women sell or barter their produce and all kinds of prepared food. The men sit in straw-covered enclosures and drink millet beer. I estimate that I could probably buy everything available in the market with my monthly social security check—well, maybe minus the goats!

Amadou makes arrangements to get me on the one available bus that is destined for Bamako via Bandiagara. I am the last one on and have to sit in the last row, with live goats squirming in sacks below my feet. I try to adjust my weight so I won't hurt the animals too much. Where is the local SPCA???

If this is what all public long-distance travel in Mali is like, I'll stay in Bamako from now on! The bus is crammed full with people, goats, chickens, plastic pails full of food stuffs, luggage. There is no escape, should there be a fire or accident. And, as if caused by my worrying, the rear wheels below me start making strange clicking noises, and a little while later there is the smell of burning rubber or oil. The driver continues driving, but then finds a place to turn off the narrow path. Everybody gets off the bus and tries to find a shady spot. The bus driver cum mechanic starts working under the bus. Thank God, someone opens the luggage compartments so that the goats and chickens loaded in there get some air. Several chickens are already in chicken heaven and are discarded.

I sit in the shade of the bus and watch the attempts at repair. A half hour, an hour, an hour and a half pass by. By about 5 p.m. I am starting to get nervous, envisioning the night on the rocks without mosquito net, without water and food, and without any local money to buy such, provided some area villagers should have mercy on us. I talk to someone from the bus company who has arrived by *moto*, apparently reached by cell phone. Bandiagara is another 28 km away, too far to walk. There is very little traffic to try hitchhiking. Most of the *motos* that pass by are already occupied by two people.

Because of road conditions, high accident rates, and little available medical care, the Peace Corps has strict prohibition against riding on motorcycles. Volunteers have been sent back to the States for breaking that rule. I don't give a damn! I will take anything motorized to get me back to Bandiagara!

One of the onlookers who had stopped on his *moto* to provide moral support sees my predicament as an opportunity to make some money and offers to take me the 28 km for the equivalent of $50. I am just about to accept his offer when a small truck comes into view. I wave furiously and it stops. The bus company employee engages in a long palaver with the driver, and after a while the driver agrees—it seems reluctantly—to take me along in the cab already occupied by two other passengers.

When we arrive in Bandiagara I tell the driver that I would like to give him something, but that the only money I have is dollars. He tells me that the lift was gratis. He even offers to bring me to the Peace Corps rest house. Unfortunately, I have no address and can't remember exactly its location. So they let me off in the center of town and I ask my way to the rest house, arriving just as night begins to fall. The guards and Emmanuel seem greatly relieved to see me, especially since I had left instructions to call in the Marines if I were not back by dark.... I get to share a tiny room with a burned-out light bulb with a young man. Given the condition of Peace Corps rest houses, I will try to avoid them in the future and find other accommodations.

Mopti

September 12

I FIND THE only bank in Bandiagara and am able to get money. I make my way to the *gare routiere* (transportation hub for buses and taxis). A young man named Gobi (he tells me that he is a guide) takes me under his wings and finds me a bush taxi (dilapidated mini-van) that goes to Mopti, my next destination. I get to sit in front with the driver. The less than 70 km take over two hours, since the vehicle has to stop often to add fresh water to the boiling radiator.

My guide book as well as Amadou had recommended the "Y a pas de Problème" Hotel in Mopti, so that is where I end up in a relatively clean room with a shower, but no sink or toilet. At lunch on the roof terrace of the hotel, Agaly shows up. He is a friend of Amadou and the owner of a *pirogue* (locally made dug-out canoe). He was alerted by Amadou via cell phone that I may be in Mopti and may be interested in taking a boat trip on the Niger. Since I am the only white female around I was easy to find....

I had hoped to find public transportation from Mopti to Djenné on the River Niger, but am told that this is only possible on Sundays during the rainy season. I am tired and have sore muscles from my trekking adventure in Dogon Country, but decide to give Agaly some business, committing to a three-hour excursion to some islands at the confluence of the rivers Bani and Niger.

Agaly picks me up at the Mopti port (the largest port

on the River Niger) in a long wooden *pirogue*, accompanied by the boatman and his "younger brother." My place is in the middle of the *pirogue* on a mat and some cushions, next to the traditional Malian tea—making equipment. I regret not having taken the motorized option, since the boatman has to work very hard to move this large monstrosity through the fast flowing, dirty waters. But I hope this way the boatman will at least be able to make some money to put food on the table for his family.

It turns out that Agaly's "younger brother" is really a vendor who unpacks his wares in the pirogue and tries to talk me into purchases between stops. We stop and tour several island villages: Kakolodaga, inhabited by Bozo fishermen; Djemedaga, inhabited by Somono *pirogue* builders; Nomidaga, inhabited by pottery makers; and the so-called Campement Touareg, where, after the Touareg upheavals in Mali in the early 1990s, only one Touareg family remains. They live from making jewelry and leather pillows for tourists.

The filth and poverty are overwhelming. Children and women beg to have their photos taken (for money), for a *cadeau* (gift) or a *biki* (ball point pen). So, obviously, I am not the first tourist to come to these villages. Some of the straw covered huts in the lower lying areas of the islands are being evacuated by the inhabitants, in anticipation of the Niger's annual flooding in October/November.

Just as we are ready to start the return trip to Mopti, dark clouds and high winds announce a huge storm. Agaly does not think it is safe to go on the water. We just make it to one of the mud houses in the vicinity before the rain starts. The house turns out to be Agaly's residence on the island: a two-room adobe residence with an empty straw covered front "room." The living room, where we sit, has no windows. The only passage for light, air and noise is the door. It is dark and awfully hot and sticky. Agaly gets a bright, battery operated lamp, as well as a plastic, hand-held fan for each of us. We hear little of the storm raging outside. The room is fairly clean and comfortable, furnished with similar upholstered furniture as I have in Bamako, a small TV (run by battery) and a coffee table. The roof and walls show signs of water leaks, but Agaly assures me that they have been repaired.

About 8 p.m. the storm has subsided and we are able to wade/slide through the flowing mud to the drenched boat man and the *pirogue*. We make the trip across the wide confluence of the Niger and Bani rivers on wet pillows in the dark night.

September 13

I had originally planned to include Djenné in my trip's itinerary, but am too exhausted. I decide to spend a second day in Mopti, taking it easy with a visit to some markets and to the mosque, accompanied by Agaly.

September 14

I have to wake up the hotel guard and the reception-ist. But to my amazement, the taxi shows up punctually at 5:30 a.m., as promised by the hotel manager, to take me to the Africa Tours Trans bus stop. My ticket, arranged by the hotel, is waiting, and the 6 a.m. departure is only thirty minutes late. The bus carries only as many passengers as there are seats. There are chickens, but they are in hard-sided cages in the luggage compartment. There is free water in sealed plastic bags. The passengers are entertained by Malian soap operas on TV. And each passenger receives a 1,000 CFA voucher (about $2.00) for lunch. There are several pit stops with questionable toilet facilities. I note that many Malian men crouch down when urinating—even those wearing western attire.

Lunch is at a huge "rest area" with a "restaurant" equipped with large tables and wooden benches. We stand in line, turn in our vouchers, and receive a plastic plate with French fries and mutton stew. There is no cutlery and I am somewhat apprehensive about using my hands that have not been washed since early morning. But the food is delicious and there is enough of it to share the leftovers with a woman who sells plastic bags full of water. Here, no food goes to waste! She thanks me in several different languages. We arrive in Bamako exactly after a ten-hour drive.

Back "home"

September 16

I AM BACK in my established routine of Bambara lessons, visits to Peace Corps office, neighborhood walks for grocery shopping, material preparation, reading, etc. I still have not heard from the Ministry of Education about part-time work before the start of the semester at the art institute. This may be moot now, since the first faculty meeting at the institute is next Monday.

At the moment, only two Cubans (Lili and Louisa) and I are living in the apartment complex. The other Cuban colleagues have returned home.

Lili, my Cuban neighbor living downstairs, knocks at my door and invites me for lunch. On a one-burner electric plate together with a pressure cooker she has prepared rice, a bean soup/sauce, fried plantain chips, and A CAKE! Delicious! This meal actually encourages me to use my four-burner bottled gas stove for something more than chili or boiled eggs.

I recommend to Lili a trip to the Dogon Country, similar to the one I just returned from. She tells me that the Cuban Embassy does not permit the Cubans to leave Bamako. So much for individual liberty!

First faculty meeting

September 19

THE ART INSTITUTE has scheduled the first faculty meeting of the fall semester. I found out about the meeting by accident. A van picks up my two Cuban neighbors, Lili and Louisa, and me a little after 7 a.m. We stop at another apartment complex in Badalabougou and pick up a third Cuban instructor. The key to his entry door had broken off and there is big palaver. We stop at a third apartment complex in Medina Coura to pick up three more Cubans, a male and two females. The places look awful, and I am relieved that I don't have to live there. Lili tells me that most of the Cubans prefer living closer to the center of town than we do, although their accommodations are considerably "more native" than ours. But nine additional Cuban instructors are expected to arrive soon, and we will most likely get company at our apartment complex as well.

We are the first faculty to arrive at the campus a little after 8 a.m. and are greeted by Bagayogo, the assistant director. He tells us the meeting will start at 8:30.

8:30 a.m., 9 a.m., 9:30 a.m., a few more people trickle in. At around 10 a.m. we are called into the "media center" and the meeting finally starts. There are about 16 individuals, equally distributed between foreigners and Malians. There is one other American: A woman in her forties who is a Fulbright scholar and will be teaching voice. The conference language is French—neither the mother tongue nor the dominant language of any one present. . . .

We introduce ourselves. There is no written agenda, though Mr. Bagayogo has his assistant hand out to each one of us three empty sheets of paper and dictates the three items he wishes to discuss: 1) the up-coming placement tests in each of the five specialty areas offered at the institute, 2) preparatory details for the semester, and 3) any other questions.

Compared with what faculty would expect at a U.S. post-secondary institution, there is no academic calendar; there are no course schedules; there is no precise enrollment information; there are no room assignments; there is no program description; there are no course descriptions or sample syllabi. I have absolutely no idea regarding the level of English proficiency of my prospective students, since I don't know what has been "taught" in the past. There are no textbooks. I request to get some guidance from the two individuals in charge of the graduate program, but they are still in Paris.

I had requested to meet the other instructor teaching English (a young Malian), who finally arrives around 11 a.m. I have difficulties understanding both his French and English. I request course outlines and a copy of the materials he uses. There are none! Mr. Bagayogo asks us to agree on our teaching schedules. My colleague suggests that he will be teaching the first and second year; I will be teaching the third year for all specialty areas as well as the two levels of the graduate program.

Faculty members have no work space or lockers for their belongings. Books, laptop, student work, etc.—you carry everything with you wherever you go. There is no website or electronic distribution list. Bagayogo tells me that I will be called on my cell phone if I need to return to the institute before the beginning of classes which have now been postponed from October 11 to October 17.

When the van leaves to bring us back to our living quarters, I still don't know definitive dates for the academic year, how many instructional days I am responsible for, how many students are enrolled in my various courses, and how I can get multiple copies made of whatever I invent as instructional materials. Supposedly, whenever it is not used for other purposes, I will be teaching in a small conference room that is equipped with a dusty TV and LCD projector. Great! I can put everything on power point.

My daughter accuses me of being too highly structured and overly organized (she calls it "too German"). I suspect that even she would be at a loss of how to proceed with so little guidance. During Peace Corps training we were repeatedly told that the most important qualities for a volunteer are to suspend American expectations of efficiency and be patient, flexible, and tolerant. I am trying!

Introduction to the English Language Club

September 23

THE PROGRAM ASSISTANT for the Peace Corps Education Program called me yesterday to tell me that Sister Rosalie, the Director of the Centre d'Etude et de Culture pour Jeunes (CECJ), would like me to come to the Center at 5 p.m. today. No other details.

I show up early since I did not know how long the taxi drive from Garantigibougou to Hamdallaye would take. I expect to meet Sister Rosalie, but she is not there. Instead I encounter a group of young people who identify themselves as members of the English Club. Apparently they would like a fluent English speaker to participate in their twice weekly meetings, Tuesday and Friday evenings from 5–8 p.m.

Most of the club members are English teachers at local schools or English students at the FLASH (Faculté de Lettres, Arts et Sciences Humaines) of the University of Bamako. Their English competence is very mixed, but they seem highly motivated and actively participate in grilling me on issues, such as "why are Americans afraid to have children?" (The average number of births for Malian women is 6.3, and a polygamous family can easily raise a football team….) "Why does America allow the death penalty?" "Why don't Americans like Moslems?"

We also discuss the benefits of early marriage (all present are single, except for two of the males). There appears to be unanimous agreement that early marriage is a good thing, "since you gain the respect of the community when you are married." I find out that to be legally married according to Malian law, you must have a civil marriage ceremony at the town hall. A religious ceremony at a mosque usually follows, but is not obligatory. If you marry only under Koranic law—and this apparently is still common in villages—neither the wife nor the children have any legal recourse in case of divorce.

Those present also confirm that the couple to be married must declare officially in writing during the civil ceremony whether their union is to be monogamous or polygamous. However, I read in a Malian newspaper some time ago, that this declaration doesn't hold much water. If the male has "the urge," he simply "marries" the object of his desire according to Moslem law. The legal wife has no recourse except grin and bear it or ask for a divorce. The latter decision usually deprives her and her children of financial support.

Moslems officially frown on sex outside of marriage (although there is prostitution in the cities). Like Elizabeth Taylor did, a self-respecting Moslem insists on marrying whomever he screws. . . .

* * *

As their annual "club project" the English Club is

planning to have a language competition for English learners at local schools, grades 7–9. The second half of the meeting is devoted to planning the event. If you are impatient with committee meetings in the U.S., don't attend such meetings in Mali!

When I raise the question of who will cover the cost for the event (e.g., for student prizes, refreshments, copying of materials, certificates, etc.), members suggest that the Peace Corps pick up the tab. But I respond with the Peace Corps' party line that it has no money. Its volunteers just offer some expertise and lots of energy. . . . I suggest club members write a formal project proposal with which we can approach the embassies of the various English-speaking countries and other organizations with an interest in English language development.

After the meeting ends, some of the club members hide me behind a wall outside the building, while one flags down a taxi and negotiates with the driver. This is done so that I will get the taxi fare that is charged the local inhabitants for the long trip home, rather than the *tubab* (white person) price I usually have to pay. I love these kids already!

A tale of dirty sheets

September 25

MOHAMED SHOWS UP for my weekly two-hour Bambara lesson, presenting me with a huge water melon as a gift. I am sharing it with Daniel and my Cuban neighbors. Delicious!

For some reason, the woman who worked at the apartment complex to do my laundry, dust, and wash the dishes has been fired. I ask Mohamed to serve as my interpreter and ask Daniel whether she will be replaced, or what I am to do about getting my laundry done. Daniel suggests a woman living across the street, but having observed her spread the "clean" laundry on the ground to dry, I decide against her.

Supposedly the woman who manages the apartment complex was to come and make a decision, but she has not yet shown up because Thursday was Malian Independence Day, Friday was declared an unofficial holiday, on Saturdays few people outside of commerce work, and Sunday, of course, is a day of rest. Daniel appears to know as little as I do. Since I am out of towels and underwear I do the laundry myself.

Washing sheets in a bucket builds character! I remember that my grandmother also did the laundry (for a family of 7) by hand, without a washing machine, and gain new respect for her generation. Of course, I also remember that during my childhood sheets were changed once monthly, a towel had to last until it actually looked dirty, and I got fresh underwear after my weekly bath in a large tin tub, placed for the event into the kitchen on Saturday afternoons.

I had planned to take a walk in the afternoon, but am prevented by a violent rain storm. I lie on the guest bed in my "study," reading, and note that hundreds of flies have migrated from the three emaciated goats tethered below my window to my fly screen, seeking protection from the rain. I spray the flies with my cockroach bomb. It works! I note that my neighbors' windows do not have fly screens—just a thin curtain that lets air flow through. From their open window below I hear Christmas music (?).

September 28

Almost three weeks after my two initial meetings at the Ministry of Education's Language Center, the promised follow-up has still not taken place. I am somewhat relieved that, apparently, I am not to train Malian pilots in English. Just to make certain there were no misunderstandings, I ask the program manager of the Peace Corps Education Sector, to give them a call and inquire whether they are still interested in my helping out. They are and I am asked to come to the Center for a third meeting to establish a schedule.

I now consider myself fully occupied: I will be teaching four courses at the art institute, one course at the CECJ, serve as participant/consultant to the CECJ's English Club six hours a week on Tuesday and Friday evenings, and will serve as conversation partner and teacher trainer at the Ministry's Language Center on Wednesday and Thursday evenings, with some formal teacher development workshops later on. This schedule will keep me out of trouble! I hope I did not bite off too much.

A visit to a primary school

October 6

I AM IN shock! It is one thing to talk about the state of public, primary education in Mali, as we did during Peace Corps training. It is another thing to experience it! I just visited the primary school, located about 200 yards from my apartment. I had seen the school previously on my neighborhood walks, but since it was vacation time there was never anyone there. Classes resumed last Monday and I thought it appropriate to introduce myself to the *directeur* (principal), a young man, named Alassane Konaté.

There are a total of 390 students in five grades, taught by four teachers: 130 precious little faces, sitting often four or five at a desk intended for two, look at me expectantly in the first grade, kept quiet by a female teacher with limited French competence. By the second grade— also taught by a woman—the number has shrunk to 82. The third grade has 81 students and is taught by a male; the fourth grade 47 (currently taught by no-one, since the principal who fills in as teacher is talking to me); and the fifth grade has 50 students, also taught by a man.

Grades one, two and three are housed in three class-rooms in an actual one-story cement building; the fourth and fifth grades are housed in a make-shift, thatched straw enclosure, separated into two "rooms" in the dusty, unfenced, overgrown school yard. The outhouse, located some 20 yards away from the school building has two stalls. I ask the principal what happens if it rains. He tells me that in case of rain the students go home. If I tell this to my grandchildren in Florida, they will want to move here....

I note that very few students have books and not all have a *cahier* (note book) in front of them to copy the words that are written by the teacher on the wooden board on the classroom wall. Some of the first graders have little black boards (similar to those I used as a first grader, but somewhat smaller, unlined, unframed, and made of wood rather than slate) in front of them and awkwardly hold stubs of chalk in their little fingers not yet used to writing utensils. I wonder how many of them own a set of crayons or a coloring book. The language of instruction is supposed to be French.

The school is the only public primary school in the large township of Kalaban-Coro /Nerekoro, a "suburb" of Bamako. I assume that all of the owners of the big houses surrounding my apartment complex send their children to private schools, and that the public school attracts mainly the children of the less affluent (if the term "affluent" can be used at all for people who expect to earn about two to three dollars a day).

The principal tells me that the school is mainly financed through the registration fees that parents have to pay once a year to enroll their children. I assume that buildings are provided and the teachers are paid by the Ministry of Education, but have to verify this in the future.

The principal sees me immediately as a possible source of help. He pleads for an additional building, for additional teachers, materials (books, notebooks, pens, pencils, blackboards, slate tablets for the lower grades). There are not even sufficient plastic canisters to contain drinking water for the children. There is no well or pump close to the school grounds that I can see. There is no place you can wash your hands.

The school day is from 8 a.m. to noon and 3 p.m. to 5 p.m. The children go home for lunch.

Here I am, a specialist in pedagogy, chock full with principles of learner-centered education, active student involvement, multi-sensory teaching, the importance of individualization and self-directed learning, etc. What in-the-hell suggestions can I make to a teacher with 130 six-, seven-, or eight-year olds, crowded in front of him or her, having to teach in a language the children do not understand or speak, and the teacher only speaks haltingly?

A smart thief

October 14

THE FOLLOWING IS a copy of the report written for Peace Corps Security at a cyber café near my apartment:

Seydou,

for the record, I would like to report the theft of my computer and camera in writing.

As I told you, on Wednesday, 10/12/11, I had an electrical problem at my apartment which caused the WiFi router, installed by Peace Corps, to malfunction. I told Daniel, the caretaker, to call a repairman. Since the repairman had not arrived by 4:30 p.m. when I had to leave for a work commitment at the Ministry of Education's Language Center, I left the key to the apartment with Daniel. When I returned from work around 8 p.m., Daniel had left, but the night guard, Samuel, returned the key to me and told me the electrical problem had been fixed.

Unfortunately, I was still unable to access the internet, so I called Peace Corps for help on Thursday. You responded very promptly by coming to the apartment, but were unable to repair the problem. You called Afribone, the wireless provider, and were told by Cisse that a technician would stop by around 9 a.m. on Friday.

On Friday, 10/14/11, a little after 8 a.m., Afribone called me and told me that the wireless antenna had been fixed. When I still could not enter the internet, he asked me to perform certain functions on my laptop (a Sony Vaio) which, however, I was not able to do. He promised to send a technician.

A little after 10 a.m., when the technician had not yet arrived, I called you to call Afribone to make certain a technician would arrive and that there was no misunderstanding.

Around 11 a.m. Daniel brought to my door a gentleman (who later told me that his name was

Drisa Traoré). When I asked him whether he came from Afribone, both he and Daniel responded affirmatively. He looked at the wireless router and noted that it was working. I took him and Daniel to my work room where my laptop was located. Daniel for some reason left the apartment. The man worked on the laptop and seemed to know what he was doing. I left the room to get him some water and was gone for a couple of minutes.

After some time, he told me that the electric outage had apparently caused some problem in the computer which he could not fix, and that the computer had to be brought to Afribone for repair. He told me that I did not need to come along, but I insisted, since I had sensitive data on the computer and did not want to let it out of sight. He told me that he worked in Afribone's office in Guarantigibougou near my apartment, however, for the work needed on my computer we had to go downtown.

On the walk from my apartment to the road [about 300 m] to catch a taxi, he wanted to return to Daniel's place because he had left his cell phone there to be recharged. I took the computer bag and waited for him on the road until he returned. I was surprised when he insisted on taking a *sotrama* downtown (he had said earlier that he had come by taxi), but not knowing Afribone or Mali business conventions, I went along. I need to state that "Drisa Traoré" was a very friendly and polite young man with good French language skills.

We arrived in central Bamako around Friday prayer time. Since thousands of men blocked the thoroughfares kneeling on their prayer mats, we had to walk round about for quite some time before we got to the place where you later found me.

Again, I was surprised that Afribone did not have any official sign to indicate its place of business, but "Drisa" told me that's where repairs were done, and the place looked indeed like a computer repair place—even though somewhat worse for the wear.

We talked to the manager who, after practicing English with me, sent us downstairs to a room where two technicians worked on my laptop for about an hour without success. We went again upstairs to the manager's office, accompanied by one of the technicians.

Since the manager's office was very small with only one chair, I went to sit in the front office. This is the first time that the laptop was out of my sight.

After about another hour (I asked for the time at 2:40 p.m.), "Drisa" came out of the manager's office and told me they were still working and he was going to get some water. He had bought some water for me earlier with his own money.

I waited for quite some time, thinking that he also went to get something to eat, since we both had missed lunch. Around 3 p.m., the technician came out of the manager's office, asking where my companion was. He told me that they had been able to repair my laptop, but that I would still not be able to use my i-pod touch (which I had still in my possession). He said that "Drisa" had put the laptop and connector into my computer bag in the manager's office before he left for water, supposedly while waiting for the bill. That is when I called you and you promptly came (which I appreciate very much!). You know the rest.

The only thing I have to add is that during the night from Friday to Saturday I discovered that my Kodak digital camera (which I kept hanging in its case on a clothes stand in the study) was also missing, as were two USB sticks. The empty camera case was still there.

I hope this helps.

Renate

Saturday, October 15

Peace Corps Security had called to tell me that Seydou would be coming to the apartment this evening with someone to look at security issues at the apartment complex.

A little after 8 p.m. I answer the door and am confronted with three superb male specimens: Seydou and two police detectives. I answer their questions and then we all go downstairs to the Cubans for their version of the event. Then they grill Daniel. The police had already taken Daniel to the police station in mid-Bamako the day before, but had released him. They search his pitiful belongings in his filthy room (intended to serve as kitchen for one of the apartments). They find nothing incriminating.

I tell Seydou that I don't think that Daniel has anything to do with the thefts. Daniel is eager to please, but he is naïve, and does not appear to be very bright. Also, he is a Bobo, and Bambara is his second language. I wonder how fluent he really is in Bambara beyond everyday language needs in order to deal with criminal matters. Being linguistically in a somewhat similar situation (i.e., having to communicate in French, my third language after English and German), I estimate that I understand about 80%-90% of what is said and am constantly searching for words.

Seydou and the two policemen take Daniel along to the police station anyway—CSI-Mali style—because they tell me that "he is constantly changing his story." I can't judge, because all the interaction with Daniel is in Bambara. I am upset.

Later that night people knock at my door to find

out what happened to Daniel. I don't open the door, but give them Seydou's phone number for more information. Given the flimsy locks at the door, I feel somewhat frightened and put "my weapon" (a beautifully carved hardwood walking stick bought at the artisan market) next to my bed. I do not sleep well.

Sunday, October 16

Daniel has not yet returned. At 9 a.m. Mohamed comes for Bambara lesson. I am too upset to focus much on Bambara, but am glad to be able to talk to someone with a Malian perspective on things.

The woman "manager" of the apartment complex arrives to find out what happened to Daniel. She says she will stop by the police department to bring him some food.

I am staying home all day and can barely concentrate to read.

Official start of semester

Monday, October 17

PICK-UP BY MINI-VAN at 7 a.m. for the one-hour ride to the institute. Nine of the 16 Cuban faculty who are to teach at the institute have not yet arrived, because—according to my Cuban colleagues—the Malian Ministry of Education has not yet sent them the funds to cover their flight expenses. While Peace Corps Volunteers are paid exclusively by the U.S. government, Cuban "volunteers" are paid exclusively by the Malian government. It goes without saying, that—given the economic situation, the low salaries and scarcity of consumer goods in Cuba—these opportunities to earn money abroad are highly prized by Cuban academics.

We have been told that there would be a start-of-semester welcoming ceremony, with invited guests from some Malian ministries and representatives of the diplomatic corps. Classes are supposed to begin at 11 a.m. There is quite a bit of police presence at the turn-off from the main road to the dirt road leading to the institute. I assume they are here because of the politicians who are expected for the opening ceremony.

I talk to both the *directeur général*, and Bagayogo, the totally overwrought and overworked assistant director in charge of academic matters, about the theft of my computer and camera and Daniel's departure for jail. They both express annoyance that Peace Corps has not informed them of the situation immediately, but that they had to find out indirectly, apparently from the night guard, after Daniel had been arrested.

At about 10 a.m. the opening ceremony begins. The expected representatives from the Malian ministries did not arrive. The only representative of the diplomatic corps is a gentleman from the Spanish embassy. The formal welcoming ceremony is a nicely done affair with an interlude of traditional Malian music. The faculty and newly-admitted students are introduced. The student body—with the exception of theater and dance majors—is heavily male dominated, but I am happy to see that each of the five departments does have some token females.

The festivities end after 11 a.m. Students crowd around a board posted in the entrance hall of the administration building where the course schedules for the semester are posted. Faculty members also stand around. Unfortunately, most of the schedules are incorrect, including mine. Bagayogo meets with the faculty present to try to make corrections. There is major confusion all around. I am finally given a copy of the hand written course schedule that was proposed two weeks ago. There will be no classes today.

The return shuttle to the apartments leaves around 1 p.m. I get off mid-town to take a *sotrama* to the Peace Corps office. Seydou wants me to accompany him to the police headquarters to make a formal deposition.

Kafka revisited!

SEYDOU AND I arrive at the police headquarters of the *1ier Arrondissement* in central Bamako at around 3 p.m. I am very pleased to see that Bagayogo, the assistant director of the institute has come as well. The huge compound is full of people, including cute little toddlers running around, apparently unsupervised. We go to a room off the courtyard, furnished with three desks, some wooden benches, and a couple of chairs. There are about a dozen people sitting and standing in the small room, including several sitting on the floor against the back wall of the office. I am the only female.

The Denzel Washington look-alike who came to my apartment on Saturday is sitting at one of the desks. He shoos away the men sitting on the bench in front of him and we take our seats.

Seydou explains that he would like the police to take a formal deposition from me, since I remembered some details which may be relevant and had not been mentioned before.

I tell my story from the beginning. A young man, apparently the court recorder, stands beside the desk and listens in, pen and paper in hand. Both he and the *commissaire* get interrupted constantly. I stop my tale of woe whenever someone interrupts them, but Seydou tells me to continue—even though they seem occupied elsewhere. He assures me that they are listening. Talk about multi-tasking!?

The detective is a stickler for exact times (at what time did Afribone call? At what time did the thief arrive? At what time did you take the *sotrama*?, etc.). Hell, I have given up paying attention to precise times since I got to Mali! I am no longer wearing a watch and depend on my cell phone if I need to check the time. I hand the detective my cell phone so that he can check the record of my incoming and outgoing calls to support my statement. He discovers a major problem. I had claimed that Cisse, the technical support person from Afribone, had called me (a statement later supported by Cisse), but the record on my cell phone indicates that I had made the call to Cisse rather than he to me, and that I apparently was on the phone for over seven minutes.

I am getting confused and somewhat distraught, since, surely I would remember if I had made the call. Would I?

I hate communicating by telephone here, since the signal often fades in and out, and I have trouble understanding, particularly if the caller speaks French. I simply can't remember this all important call. The detective tells me that the cell phone record is definitive proof that the call was made from my phone. Allah, the Merciful! What else don't I remember or what else do I remember incorrectly? Was it someone else who called me? For some reason Cisse's phone record cannot be checked.

Other people come and sit around the desk. When Bagayogo asks whether Daniel can also be asked to tell his version in our presence, I suddenly note that one of the three or four men who had been sitting on the floor at the back wall is Daniel. I conjecture that these poor creatures are in custody awaiting formal charges. Daniel gets up and takes a seat at the bench next to us. With Bagayogo as interpreter, I ask Daniel whether he needs money or food?

People come and go, and some join around our table. Black faces are difficult to recognize in dim light and I am not really watching them. But suddenly I become aware that two of the men are the manager and technician from the computer repair shop where my laptop was stolen, and I assume correctly that the remaining crowd (at least half a dozen) is from Afribone. The detective makes me retell my version of the story. They listen and answer some questions. They all speak French and support each other. No wonder that Daniel can't compete with these city slickers and therefore has become the scapegoat for this affair.

I wonder whether in the U.S. it is also customary to have all parties involved in a criminal case present at the depositions. I can't remember that from watching CSI— my information source for criminal procedures. . . . Obviously, in this case, they hear the various versions and can adjust their own to fit their needs. I also vaguely remember that there is a limit in the U.S. for how long a suspect can be kept in detention without formal charge. I think it is 48 hours, but am not sure whether there is such a limit in Mali. I got to get Daniel out of here!

The "court recorder" brings me a handwritten statement for my signature—supposedly containing my deposition. I read it to the extent that I can decipher the handwriting and find many discrepancies, indicating that Malian police officers are no better at multi-tasking then I am. . . . I try to correct the most relevant errors and sign the statement.

Some people leave, some stay. I ask to speak to the detective in private. I tell him that I am convinced that Daniel had little if anything to do with the theft and could he please be released. I repeat that I just don't think he is bright enough, and that I doubted his language competence to deal with this situation. Daniel is trying to please, and tells the police what he thinks they want to hear.

Both the detective and Seydou are opposed to the release, "because he changes his story." Bagayogo tells me that they are sure Daniel will talk if he is beaten. Hell, if you beat me, I will confess to the theft myself!!!

The detective tells me that he considers Daniel a flight risk and asks me if I can vouch for him and produce him, if needed. By now, I am so desperate that I agree to this, and I appear to have convinced the detective. But when it comes to signing the release papers, thanks to Allah, it is Bagayogo who is signing the release papers rather than me. Apparently there is no bail.

Daniel and I are driven back to the apartment in a Peace Corps vehicle. He is welcomed by the night guard and my two Cuban colleagues, one of whom weeps and hugs Daniel and me in gratitude for his return.

Another night with sleep problems.

The life of a working stiff

Tuesday, October 18

I AM TO meet my first classes today. Thanks to Allah, I had given print-outs of my syllabus and some other materials to Bagayogo a week ago to be copied for the beginning of the semester or I would have lost these materials too—together with all my other work that was stored on my stolen computer, such as power-point presentations, resource material, texts and exercises laboriously constructed or collected over the past two months.

The two-hour class for multi-media majors is supposed to start at 8 a.m. The door to the room where I am to teach is locked. I go to Bagayogo who opens it for me and turns on the AC. I get to teach in the TV and LCD-equipped room which, of course, is a useless advantage now, since I no longer have a laptop which I can connect to the LCD projector.

Four students come in by 8:15 and I start to teach.

Slowly others trickle in, and by 9 a.m. there are nine students (all male), with eight apparently still missing. I never do get the list of enrollments on which I am to keep an attendance record. Each time a new student comes in, I interrupt what we are doing and I give him the syllabus and information form to complete for my own records.

The English proficiency of the students present is very mixed. This is supposedly third year English, but most students are at a total loss, and many clearly have major problems understanding anything I say, although the majority of those present have had English at secondary school as well as at the institute. I will have to lower my expectations for what we will be able to accomplish this semester. Maybe things will improve, once students get used to my accent.

I need to use the small, free-standing (shaky) white board available, but it is still filled with writing from the spring semester. There is no rag to wipe the board and there are no writing utensils. I interrupt Bagayogo in his office and he equips me with two used markers and some Kleenexes. The Kleenexes do not work, since the ink has penetrated the white board in the three intervening months. Bagayogo comes again and together with a student scrubs the white board.

Why were all these routine preparatory details not taken care of during the summer? Why does it take an assistant director to do these things? What are the regular duties of the maintenance crew and who is in charge? Why have enrollment lists not been finalized? All students have to pass annual exams to be admitted or readmitted to the institute. So it is not that students are storming in at the last minute to be registered. Why is there still no dependable teaching schedule with room assignments?

I dismiss the class at 9:50 a.m. and wait for the beginning of the second class which is to start at 10. I wait until 10:30, but no one shows up. I finally interrupt Bagayogo in a meeting and am told that the masters level students who are scheduled with me for that hour have not yet arrived. I go to the media center to use the internet, but the internet connection is down. I wait until after noon, when the shuttle leaves to bring us back to our residences. Patience has never been one of my virtues, but this is ridiculous! If I would be paid at a consultant rate for all the time wasted while waiting, I could really live in style!

* * *

I stop at the Peace Corps Office to use the internet. Seydou tells me that I will probably be moved out of my current residence for security reasons. I stay at the office until my 5 p.m. commitment with the English Club at CECJ.

The first members of the Club trickle in by 5:45 p.m. and we have another one of the chaotic meetings trying to plan an inter-school English language competition. Decisions made at one meeting are not recorded, and the information gets lost between meetings. People not present at previous meetings object to decisions made during those meetings, etc.

In my frustration I am tempted to take over and make the arrangements for the Club. I have organized language fairs and competitions before, and it is really not that difficult, once you have a step-by-step plan. But doing things for them will not help third-world development. Things have to be accomplished "the Malian way" to have any hope of lasting impact.

I am somewhat short tempered tonight and tell Club members that I will no longer attend their meetings regularly, but that they should tell me when they want me to come and for what specific purpose.

At night, back in my apartment, I still have difficulties sleeping.

Looking for new digs

Wednesday, October 19

I AM ASKED to come to the Peace Corps office to explore alternative housing possibilities. The Peace Corps expects that the agencies that request volunteers make some in-kind contributions for volunteer service. I fully support this Peace Corps policy, because the tendency in Mali— as well as in the rest of the developing world—is often to expect that things are done for them, free of charge and without commitment on their part. The art institute's contribution for getting my services is to provide housing.

The problem is that the institute has only one vacant unit outside the apartment complex where I am now living. It is located in a huge, older apartment complex in Medina Coura and houses four other Cuban instructors and numerous Malian civil servants and teachers with their families, as well as the occasional goat.

We go to look at the place, making our way through drying laundry, plastic pails, and cooking braziers, up the stairs to a third floor end unit: The walls definitely need a paint job. The small refrigerator does not work. None of the light bulbs work. The toilet does not flush.

The only aspect I prefer of this apartment to my present residence is its location: It is much closer to the institute and to central Bamako than my place in Guarantigibougou/Nerekoro—where, during rush hour, it can take over an hour to get across one of the two bridges spanning the huge expanse of the Niger river that divides Bamako into two parts. I agree to take the apartment, provided the necessary repairs are done.

In the evening I tell my two Cuban colleagues downstairs of the proposed move. They warn me of security problems at the Medina Coura apartment complex as well. I am pleased that the Peace Corps' American assistant director wants to have security check out the place before a final decision is made.

A visit to the U.S. Embassy

Thursday, October 20

I HAVE AN appointment with the Assistant Cultural Attaché at the U.S. Embassy who also doubles as education officer. On my taxi drive to the embassy, I see thousands of school children—some with little flags—lining the streets together with some adults (probably their teachers), and many, many police. The taxi driver explains that the president of the Ivory Coast is visiting Mali and will be driven along this same route. I wonder whether West African friendship and development would not be better served leaving these children in school, rather than disrupting their education for hours while standing in the hot sun, just to wave for a couple of seconds to a passing, visiting head of state. But a display of pomp and pageantry takes precedence over my considerations.

The U.S. Embassy is an island of cleanliness and calm. The only negative aspect is the lengthy security procedure. The young Marine can barely keep up recording all the visitors—mostly Malians who are definitely better dressed and look less sweaty than the Americans present. Through long corridors I am led to the appropriate office.

The purpose of my visit is to put the institute on the embassy's list as a site for any U.S. cultural events they bring to Mali. I also want to explore possible assistance in creating an English Club at the institute, as well as inquire about resources for my teaching. And finally, I want to "grease the wheels" for funding of the proposal for the inter-school English language competition that the English Club will submit to the embassy via Sister Rosalie. I am pleased to hear about all kinds of possibilities for collaboration and I offer them my services in the area of teacher development, if desired. I also get to meet the Public Affairs Officer, an ex-Peace Corps Volunteer who served in Ivory Coast.

In the afternoon, together with Seydou of Peace Corps Security, and the assistant coordinator for the Education sector we make another trip to inspect my potential future living quarters for a security check. We have to wait almost an hour, before Bagayogo finally shows up with the keys. No repairs appear to have been started. Seydou approves the apartment, and Peace Corps promises to install some fly screens for the doors and window. Bagayogo even commits to a possible paint job, but I am not holding my breath. Supposedly I will be moved early next week. I am not to tell anyone of the impending move, but, of course, the Cubans know already.

A moving experience
Sunday, October 27

THIS LAST WEEK has been a turbulent week without any time for journal entries. Here is the week in review:

As nothing really happens on time here, I was not surprised when the move to my new quarters, planned for Saturday October 22, did not happen. But ever the optimist, I was fully packed and waiting.

On the 22nd I was told I would be moved on Monday, October 24. On Monday morning I went to the institute for my teaching duties and experienced pretty much a repeat of the chaos and disorganization encountered during the previous week. The 8 a.m. course had been cancelled because many students had been taken to town for a musical event. The 10 a.m. class was attended by only half of the students on my enrollment list.

I cancelled my afternoon plans to attend a workshop for English teachers offered through the U.S. Embassy and returned to Guarantigibougou, because I expected to be moved. The Peace Corps office called late afternoon to tell me that the move had been postponed to the next day.

On Tuesday, October 25, my courses at the institute still experienced scheduling and room assignment problems. Apparently, I no longer get to teach in the LCD-projector equipped room. And the room in the neighboring building I used before was also occupied by another teacher. I took the few students who showed up to the media center and we were joined by two of the Cuban instructors who want to refresh their English language skills.

I talked to the director of the institute and asked him when the refrigerator and TV would be delivered that were the apparent cause for the delay in moving me. He assured me that it would happen that afternoon and I would be moved later that day.

I again returned to Guarantigibougou and waited for the pick-up truck, sitting for a fourth day among my packed boxes and suitcases. By now I had emptied the refrigerator and finished whatever food was in the apartment. When I called to confirm the move, I was told that the move had been postponed until Wednesday, and that I should call Bagayogo at 9 a.m. the next day to confirm things.

On Wednesday, October 26, I again stayed home. I gave Bagayogo a call at 9 a.m., only to be told that the director had not yet arrived to approve the purchase of the refrigerator and TV, and that Bagayogo would call me back around 10. No call! I waited until 4:30 p.m., getting angrier by the minute. I sent a text message to Peace Corps to let them know that I was really getting quite discouraged. The coordinator of the education sector called me a little after 5 p.m., apparently alerted by my message to his assistant. By now I was livid! I told him that I have had it, and that he had 24 hours to either get me moved, find me a new work site or send me back to the States.

Ten minutes later I got a call from Bagayogo, apparently alerted by the Peace Corps. I am really angry and tell him that I have had to cancel other work commitments because of the expected move, that the treatment I was getting showed no respect for me, my work or my time, and that I have had it. Unfortunately, I am not the most articulate person in French, and definitely not when I am mad. . . . But he got the message and arrived with his personal pick-up and a helper after dark around 7 p.m. to move my belongings. When I express dismay that it falls to the second in command at the institute to perform moving duties, I am told there was no one else. What about all the healthy-looking males at the front gate, sitting around drinking tea on many occasions? Will I ever understand this culture?

Unfortunately, because of my gas stove and the additional furniture I had acquired (a book case and two small desk-tables), not everything fits onto the double-cab pick-up. So I would have to face another trip the following day.

I barely had enough energy to negotiate one set of stairs with all my junk in Guarantigibougou (books, dishes, pots and pans, clothes, bedding, etc.—much of it in plastic bags because I had no boxes), but arriving in Medina Coura we had to negotiate two sets of stairs (44 steps!) to get to the third floor of my new apartment.

Bagayogo and his helper left around 10 p.m. I was absolutely exhausted, but couldn't sleep. The place was infested with mosquitoes, but my mosquito net was still in Guarantigibougou.

On Thursday, October 27 I spent the morning trying to clean the filthy place and accommodate my personal belongings in the one armoire in the bedroom. I also attended a session of the workshop for English teachers at a near-by technical school. Interesting experience!

Although Bagayogo promised that my remaining things would be moved on Thursday, I didn't really expect anything to happen. But I definitely did not want to spend another night without mosquito net! So, around 1 p.m. I took a taxi back to Guarantigibougou and loaded it up with everything left there except the furniture.

The taxi had just returned with me and my belongings to the new apartment, when—lo and behold—a driver showed up in a small truck. I did the 40-minute trip back to Guarantigibougou for a second time that afternoon, and we picked up my remaining possessions. By 5:30 p.m. I finally had all my possessions in one place, but I had missed the festivities at the National Park to celebrate 50 years of USAID presence in Mali.

My new living quarters

As I NO longer have a camera to take pictures of my new

residence, I will describe it instead: You come up the paved road, past the oldest girls school in Bamako, and immediately after the large school compound you turn into a huge, unpaved, sandy lot that is used mornings and evenings by the nearby stationed soldiers for exercise and football practice. You arrive at a large, three-storied, 27-unit apartment building that must have been built after Malian independence, in the 1970s. The complex is divided into three sections, with nine apartments in each section (three on each floor). You climb the stairs of the first section to the end unit on the last floor, overlooking the dusty "football field" below.

From the narrow outside walkway—hanging full of drying laundry—you enter the narrow hallway of my apartment through an ill-fitting wooden screen door (installed by Peace Corps) and a hard-to-close louvered steel door. Immediately on the right is the small kitchen cubicle (no cupboards, but thanks to Allah there is a sink next to a cement slab); opposite on the left is the bathroom, equipped with ill-fitting plumbing, including a bidet. There is no toilet seat; the sink wobbles when you lean against it; and the back of the bidet has a pile of soggy rags stuffed in it, which I have not yet had the courage to remove to examine why they are there. The water pipes that run along the walls are covered by layers of dried muck and appear to be ready for an archeological excavation. My most appreciated luxury is that during my first week of residence here there has only been one water outage, and the water pressure and quality (no rust!) is definitely better than in my former residence.

From the short hallway you enter my large, high-ceil-inged *salon* (living room), with a chipped, yellow and red, checkerboard tiled floor that shows years of wear and tear, as do the dirty yellow walls. The *salon* is furnished with a dusty, dark grey couch, a love seat and two arm chairs—all having seen better and cleaner days—surrounding a coffee table which apparently had been left out in the rain for quite some time before it ended up at my residence. There are also a round, wobbly dining table, two wobbly chairs, a rough book case (made by my personal carpenter in Garantigibougou), a miniature refrigerator, and another book-case-like structure made from rattan and covered by a curtain, which serves as my pantry and kitchen cabinet. In the corner stands my non-working TV. One window of the *salon* overlooks the impromptu football practice field below, but I never open the louvered steel shutters because of the dust. Two louvered steel doors (with very ill fitting wooden screen doors) lead out to a private balcony over-looking the tops of trees. The foliage is so dense that you can only see a small slice of the dirt yard below from the balcony's edge. If it were not for the traffic noise, the dust, the mosquitoes, and the heat, I would spend most of my time out there.

From the living room you enter the one, good-sized bedroom, also with access to the balcony, furnished with two single beds (one with mosquito netting), two night stands, an armoire, my hand-made wobbly desk and a wobbly chair. The bedroom has an air conditioning unit—which, unfortunately, is pretty useless, since there is no glass in the windows and doors, and whatever cool air it can muster to produce escapes through the slats of the louvered door coverings. Each room is lit by a neon tube which barely provides enough light to cut your finger nails.

The apartment complex is inhabited by a number of Cuban colleagues and Malian government employees and teachers. Quite a few of the Malians own cars, so these appear to be middle class residences.

Approximately 30 yards directly opposite the large apartment complex where I am living is a low building with half a dozen garage-like units (that is, in fact, what they were supposed to be) where reside the poor folks, without electricity and individual water faucets. They do all their cooking and most everything else outside in the yard. On "my side of the tracks" most people speak at least some French; on the opposite side I can't communicate with anyone.

The tale of the forged CFA bill

Friday, October 28

A COUPLE OF days ago I ended up with a counterfeit 10,000 CFA bill (about $20). I go to my bank—the Banque Nationale de Développement Agricole—to exchange it, because I am convinced I got the forged bill from its ATM machine the week before. After a lengthy wait and discussions with several different bank employees, I am told that it is impossible that I got the counterfeit bill at one of their machines, since all bills disbursed by machine are automatically checked. I am told that I got duped by a merchant, who used me to get rid of the bill. Here is what must have happened: I gave the bill to pay for lunch at one of the Lebanese-owned restaurants in town. The waiter returned the bill to me, telling me it was counterfeit. Even the owner of the restaurant stopped by my table to tell me that the bill was no good, and that I should return it to the bank. According to the bank employee, the merchant or waiter must have taken my good 10,000 CFAs that I had got from the bank's ATM and returned the worthless bill. Oh well, it is only money. . . . But from now on, I will mark all my large bills to avoid this happening again.

In the afternoon I go to the Peace Corps office to try to catch up on e-mail and submit the claim forms for the computer and camera thefts.

Asifa and David (also a retired university professor), a volunteer couple closer to my age who are staying at the Peace Corps Transit House for a weekend respite have invited me to come along to a Moroccan restaurant for dinner. Great place! Great meal! Good company, though together with three young American NIH workers we are the only guests on this Friday evening.

A pleasant week-end

Saturday, October 29

ASIFA AND DAVID want to have a picnic at the National Park near my new residence and I decide to join them. To my surprise, when we meet at the entry to the park, they bring along David, a young volunteer from my own group, who had been brought to Bamako by Peace Corps van to recover from malaria. He is the first person in my group of volunteers to suffer from that awful sickness. He is still pretty weak, but no longer has the high fever, chills, muscle aches and headaches that come with that disease. I hope my malaria prophylaxis works better than his....

The National Park, which also houses the National Museum and a gorgeous—though extremely pricey—restaurant must be the loveliest place in all of Mali. Trees! Green grass! Flowers! No garbage! Well-maintained walkways—well worth the 1,500 CFAs entry for foreigners (as opposed to 300 CFAs that Malians have to pay). We sit in the shade and consume a bottle of red, together with French bread, cheese, paté, and water melon. This is how life should be!

The life of a working stiff, continued

Monday, October 31

THIS IS THE beginning of the third week of classes at the institute. I still have only met with one half of my students. There are still problems with room assignments, and I again end up in the media center to teach—without a board to write on. Our small group is surrounded by talking people who are not part of the class. This is really frustrating!

Tuesday, November 1

Nothing new at the institute! For some reason I get to teach in the technology equipped room today. No wonder students don't show up. They don't know where class will be, unless they come searching. . . . The graduate students I am to start teaching today don't show up. Frankly, I no longer give a damn!

Wednesday, November 2

I am attending a workshop for English teachers on communicative language teaching, offered through the auspices of the American Embassy. The instructor is an ex-Peace Corps volunteer who is working at present as an education consultant with the Ministry of Education in Togo. She is in town for two consecutive weeks, giving one-week-long workshops to two different groups of teachers. There are about 40 Malian English teachers attending. I am sitting next to a woman, totally covered in black—including black gloves—, except for her eyes. As sign of fashion consciousness she is, however, wearing white, high heeled sandals over the black stockings covering her feet.

I find it somewhat disconcerting to interact with the totally veiled woman, because the veil covering her face muffles her voice, and I lack those additional facilitators of communication, such as lip movement and facial expressions, to determine whether she is friend or foe.

The English competence of most of the participants is quite good, but it is interesting to watch the interactions. The men who constitute the majority of those attending definitely dominate discussion. The women practically never raise their hands to respond, and do not talk unless directly addressed. Although the instructor valiantly attempts to involve all participants through pair-work or small group work, I wonder how much actually "sinks in." The major point of contention—necessitating lengthy discussion—is that the letter format handed out to participants as a model for English business letter writing does not follow the model in their textbook....

I hear that the students who usually attend the technical school where the workshop is held have gone on strike in order to prepare for the upcoming Tabaski holiday which will be either on Sunday or Monday. The Ministry in charge of determining such things has not yet announced the definite date for the holiday. Apparently, I am the only one who finds it unusual that holiday preparations serve as valid reason for a strike.

Thursday, November 3

Another day at the English teachers' workshop. I spend the afternoon at the Peace Corps office, catching up on e-mail and fighting the bureaucracy pertaining to my computer and camera theft report.

In the evening I am washing my laundry (sheets, towels and all), using a bucket and the bidet, and hang it to dry on my balcony. My hands itch something terrible after using the sharp laundry soap. I will definitely have to get myself another laundry woman. I already did find a new ironing man in the neighborhood as well as a couple of *butigis* where I can get the basic necessities.

Friday, November 4

Some of the education volunteers in rural areas are

working with local English teachers, trying to improve their teaching skills. Since few of the volunteers are trained teachers, they often lack the knowledge or skills to work effectively with their Malian counterparts. Peace Corps has asked me to give a presentation to my young colleagues on "what to look for in effective language teaching" during the upcoming in-service training session for my group of volunteers. I am staying home to draft an outline.

I spend the afternoon again at the Peace Corps office on the computer. At 5 p.m. it is back to the English Club at the CECJ where, this time, only six members showed up to help plan the interschool English language competition, scheduled for mid-January. I am somewhat apprehensive, since I recommended the event to the U.S. Embassy for funding. My reputation is on the line, and I am not sure the Club can pull it off. So, far, I have drafted all documents (invitation letter, tentative program, outline for various competitions, evaluation criteria, budget, etc.). Organization is definitely not the strengths of those present.

At 8 p.m., Hillary, the American Fulbright scholar at the institute, has invited me for dinner and a glass of wine at the French Cultural Center. The Center has a small restaurant and offers all kinds of exhibits, movies, musical and other cultural events. What a great little island of western ambiance! I will definitely return.

Of Cuban-American friendship

Saturday, November 5

MOHAMED, MY BAMBARA instructor, comes to my new place of residence for Bambara lessons and invites me to come to his house on Sunday to celebrate Tabaski. I am looking forward to it!

* * *

I call on a Cuban colleague who lives in the apartment complex to help me connect my still non-working TV. Unfortunately, he is also not able to get the equipment to work. Before leaving the apartment he tells me that he has no problem with helping me, but I should not request his help in front of other Cuban colleagues, particularly not in front of "la Noire" (while a number of my Cubans colleagues have some African ancestry, she definitely is the darkest). Apparently the Cuban embassy frowns on any contact my colleagues have with Americans, and "la Noire" serves as embassy liaison. He assures me that as far as he is concerned, he has only disagreements with the American government, but not with the American people. I am sad, that I won't be able to party with the Cubans in my new residence. I hope I will find some Malian friends in the neighborhood.

Half an hour later, one of the female Cubans knocks on my door and brings me a bowl of soup. I invite her in but she is not staying. The Cubans at Guarantigibougou definitely were more friendly—maybe because "la Noire" was not living in the same place protecting her charges from American influence....

Tabaski

Sunday, November 6

I HAVE TWO invitations to celebrate the feast of Tabaski: one from Mohamed, my Bambara instructor and general trouble shooter, and one from Abdoulaye, the president of the CECJ English Club. When I leave to find a taxi to go to Mohamed's house around 9 a.m., the cow and three sheep that have been tethered to trees to await their sacrificial slaughter for the Tabaski celebration since yesterday are still tethered below my apartment. They tug on the ropes fastened around their necks to forage amid the garbage left by residents, not realizing that the end is near. Mohamed later explains to me that the cow is a non-traditional Tabaski sacrifice, but has apparently been bought instead of the traditional sheep, to be shared by several families. When I return from my outing several hours later, the animals are gone.

Tabaski is the holiday commemorating Abraham's willingness to sacrifice his son in response to Allah's command. I am happy to hear that Allah relented and had him sacrifice a sheep instead. Therefore, any self-respecting Malian Muslim family celebrates the holiday and Allah's mercy by killing at least one sheep.

When I arrive at Mohamed's house, their sheep has already been killed and skinned, and Boubakar, the son, has started to cut up parts of the animal on a piece of cardboard on the ground outside the gate of the house. The head of the large-horned animal, as well as the skin, wait next to the door, to be picked up by tanners roaming the neighborhood. A hole had been dug in front of the neighbor's house to catch the blood of the neighborhood sacrifices. The hole also holds the contents of the intestines and whatever else of the carcasses that is inedible. I am sorry that I did not come in time for the sacrificial killing, but am told that I would not have been able to watch anyway, since women do not take part in the slaughtering.

Mohamed and I sit in lawn chairs inside the compound, near the large entry door, while his son and his wife sit on little stools and cut up the sheep into little pieces. The two daughters and the family maid scurry around, sweeping and starting to prepare the meal. Another big sheep (a Tabaski gift of one of the daughters to her mother) is tied up nearby to be slaughtered the next day.

Every couple of minutes someone stops by the door. Sometimes it is a blind beggar led by a boy or woman, sometimes a person who appears to be known to the family. All are given some meat. Groups of children also stop by and are given money coins. A number of neighbors enter the court yard to exchange lengthy blessings in Bambara. I join in with "amina" (Amen) every time I hear the word "Allah," since that is the only word I understand of the many ritualistic good wishes that are uttered.

Mohamed has explained to me that on Tabaski it is customary to ask neighbors, friends, and family members for forgiveness for anything one may have done to irritate them. Mohamed tells me that even if the person is not sincere with his or her apology, and even if the recipient of the apology is reluctant to accept it, your misdeeds will be forgiven by Allah. Just in case, I also apologize to the family members for anything offensive I may have done. I like this practice! It is much more civilized than a catholic confession....

Mohamed takes off with a neighbor to visit nearby houses for Tabaski greetings. I am somewhat at a loss as to what to do. Mohamed's wife suggests I sit in the *salon* to escape the flies.

I note that the family has acquired new upholstered furniture since my last visit, each of the four pieces decorated with a crocheted doily. Around noon one of the daughters brings me a plate with grilled sheep liver and some pieces of meat. Just when I finish it, Mohamed returns and is also given a plate. I am not sure whether this is the extent of the Tabaski meal, but since I am supposed to visit another family later today, I excuse myself around 1 p.m. to give the family members a rest before they will go on their afternoon visitations that are customary on that day.

For my second invitation later that afternoon, I have arranged with Abdoulaye to meet at the Center where the English Club usually meets. There are no street names where he lives and his compound is hard to find. He comes to the Center on his scooter, and for a second time since taking the oath of office as a Peace Corps volunteer I commit the cardinal sin (as declared by Peace Corps administration), to ride on a motor cycle. Since I am wearing Malian attire today and am having difficulties climbing on the scooter with my tight wrapper, I am more concerned with my uncovered legs than with my uncovered (helmetless) head.

Abdoulaye is about my daughter's age and lives with his family (one wife and three children), his parents and several brothers and sisters and their families in a small compound, each family having a room surrounding the cemented court yard. There is a common water faucet next to the entrance door to the compound. Abdoulaye's father is my age, his mother about ten years younger but showing the wear and tear of giving birth to and raising eight children.

After Mohamed's relatively westernized, middle class Malian neighborhood, Abdoulaye's compound offers quite a contrast. Since he is a university graduate and works as a school administrator, I did not expect to get transported back to surroundings which are similar to those I experienced during my pre-service training stay in the village.

Abdoulaye's parents speak neither French nor English. But I am greeted very warmly. Since my Malian last name is Diarra, the same as their's, the ice is broken quickly despite the lack of a common language and I am declared a family member. I am served water (from the communal cup) and a sweet, ginger flavored drink as well as some skewers of grilled sheep from the family's sacrificial offering. I note that the meat is cold and send an emergency prayer to Allah, hoping that it had not been the resting place of the many flies buzzing around. . . . Abdoulaye excuses himself to pray, and I occupy myself with the cute children who examine me. One little girl is obviously petrified by my albino-like, blotchy looking, straight haired appearance and starts crying.

Abdoulaye's parents declare that Malian people my age are less fit than I am. They appear sorry that I have only one child. Even Abdoulaye has problems understanding how one can voluntarily limit one's family to only one child. He tells me that Malian men want as many children as Allah gives them. I do not ask him whether the women share that same desire. I also refrain from asking whether Allah sends a monthly support check or pays the school fees.

Abdoulaye wants to show me his school and introduce me to his in-laws and his wife, who—despite the holiday—has apparently decided to flee the overpopulated compound and go to her small *butigi* selling beauty products.

I am introduced to many neighbors, listen to umpteen blessings, and engage in "joking cousin" banter with the Traorés. It is customary for the Diarras and Traorés to malign each other in a joking fashion, each one claiming to be better than the other.

Abdoulaye's sister, Mariam, has joined us, as well as his precious two-year old daughter who is trustingly holding on to my hand. Mariam tells me that her "husband" is working in Finland. She was married to him in absentia several years ago when she was 16 and has not seen him. A very effective method of birth control....

When it starts to get dark, Abdoulaye and Mariam find me a taxi for the trip back to Medina Coura.

Impenetrable cultural secrets

- While riding the *sotrama* (mini-vans with seats replaced by wooden benches around the sides, used for public transportation), I noticed that the children riding with their mothers (rarely with their fathers) are unbelievably well behaved. No squirming in the tight quarters, no crying, little if any talking. They sit on their mothers' laps, sleeping or looking with big eyes at the *tubabu* or the world around. American children in a similar context would squirm, try to get up, scream, cry, talk or at least insist on being entertained by those around them. Why do children behave so differently here? They can't be all lacking energy because of malnutrition (though 27% of the children are believed to suffer from nutritional deficiencies), and they can't all have parasites (though it is estimated that 50% of children do!).

- Why do the majority of Malian women have such lovely, flawless skin, despite sub-Saharan climate conditions? Is it because they use less soap than we do? Is the reason the *Beurre de Karité* (shea butter products) many women use by the gallon? (I bought some, but it is very greasy and I note no difference). Or are they just genetically favorably endowed?

- Many behavior patterns differ noticeably between Mali and the U.S. For example, already when my grandchildren were toddlers they were shushed when "Oma is talking" and told to wait their turn. But many Malian adults have no problem interrupting a conversation for a cell phone call, and they do not hesitate to walk up and interrupt someone else's conversation. Why do we find such behaviors irritating, but they apparently don't?

- Why can Malian youngsters as young as six years of age be expected (and able) to carry around on their backs their younger siblings most of the day or regularly fetch wood or water, while American youngsters can't be expected to tidy up their rooms?

- Teens play soccer below my apartment in the huge sandy lot. They wear no distinguishable, common piece of clothing for either team, not even socks, t-shirts, etc. How do they or the spectators know which player plays on which team?

A visit

Sunday, November 13

THIS MORNING, MARIAM, a member of the English Club and the Club's president's sister, came to visit me to get some help with a presentation on women's rights which she is to give to students at *a lycée*, as part of her preparation as an English teacher. She arrives on her *moto*, but, unfortunately, has forgotten her notes at home. I had given her an article in a recent *National Geographic* magazine which I found lying around in the Peace Corps office. The article reported on the change in family size in Brazil in the span of one generation, and how the education of women was a major factor in that change.

I had hoped that Mariam would conclude that, literally, keeping Malian women barefoot and pregnant, rather than guaranteeing them literacy and an education, was the main obstacle to women's rights in Mali, but I am not sure that she is convinced. She is a devout Moslem and (like devout Catholics, Mormons or Jews) probably shares the Prophet Mohammed's (or other religions's) covert intention that the ranks of the believers be increased as much and as fast as possible. "Go forth and multiply!"

Come to think of it, the Brazilian experience of reduced family size is not so much different from the experience in the western world. The difference is, that it came about fifty years later.

In my own family in Germany, for instance, both my mother and father came from families with six (live) children. In my parents' generation, family size ranged from one to four children; in my own generation, only one cousin has three children, the others one or two.

Of course, the industrial revolution, the demographic change from agricultural life to life in cities, and the two World Wars had a lot to do in discouraging large families, but so did the development of social security systems (which helped to support older parents so that they did not have to rely solely on their children for support in old age), the education and increasing equality of women, and improved methods of birth control. And my generation witnessed women's liberation and "the pill" which finally gave women who were so inclined decision making power as to family size.

Maybe in another fifty years, Mali—with its current rate of births per woman of 6.4—will be where Brazil is today, with 1.9 children per woman. The question is, however, whether Mali (or other developing countries) has fifty years to manage its population. What about water, food, education, fuel, jobs, health care, social services and the rest of the infrastructure required to support an increasing population?

It cannot just be Muslim doctrine and attitudes which are an obstacle to population control. A number of predominantly Moslem countries have clearly become aware of the relationship between family size, development, and standard of living. Thus, for instance, Iran—with an average number of birth per woman of 1.8 children, Turkey and Tunesia—with an average number of 2.1 children, Morocco and Indonesia—with an average number of 2.4, and even Oman—with 2.6 certainly don't follow the example of their parents' generation.

* * *

It appears that many Malians have not developed western sensitivities when it comes to overstaying their welcome. After three hours of tea and cookies, after all conversation topics are exhausted, after penetrating periods of silence, after thoroughly exploring the reading materials on the coffee table, after clear indicators of tiredness by the hostess, Mariam does not take the cue that it is time to leave. She arrived at 10 and it is now 1 p.m. But a little after 1 p.m. I get a call from some of my young Peace Corps colleagues who have arrived in Bamako for the two weeks of inservice training that is to begin on Monday in Tubaniso. They have met for lunch at a local restaurant and invite me to join them. Delighted to have a legitimate excuse to terminate Mariam's visit, I tell her that I have to leave now.

I have to reflect, however, on one thought-provoking comment made by Mariam. She does not share my admiration for family cohesiveness. She feels that many of her countrymen are lazy or unambitious because they expect the extended family to take care of them even if they don't contribute. Ann Landers' occasional advice to "throw the bum out" (i.e., an irresponsible child) is seldom followed in Malian culture.

Am I losing it?—Part One

Monday, November 14

THE DRY SEASON has definitely begun. The early mornings are delightfully cool. I even use a sheet to cover myself. I regularly hear the faint call of the muezzin around 5 a.m., but somehow I never before heard the 5:30 reveille of the nearby army barracks. Does sound carry better in dry air?

An hour later a large group of soldiers does their morning run through the *quartier.*

The van which is supposed to pick up the instructors in time for the 8 a.m. courses at the institute arrives at the apartments 45 minutes late. When my 8 o'clock course begins shortly before 9, I actually have most of the enrolled students present. The group behaves as unruly as a bunch of 6th graders and I yell at them. Never before in my long career teaching in the U.S., in Nigeria, in Mexico, in Colombia, in Germany have I lost composure before a group of adult students! Am I losing it?

The previous Thursday I had written a letter to Bagayogo, reiterating—what I had told him on several occasions—that after the fourth week of classes I still had not yet encountered one half of my students, and that it was very difficult to constantly re-teach previously covered materials to new arrivals. I also asked for recommendations on how I could give a common test to students who didn't attend classes or attended only sporadically.

In the U.S. I would have dropped students from the class register after four unexcused absences. In the U.S. it would badly reflect on me as a teacher, if half of my students failed a test—which will surely happen here. *Insha Allah*, one of these days I will adjust to higher education Malian style and accept without frustration the local concept of time and responsibility.

Bagayogo was clearly not happy with the letter. Both he and his assistant show impatience with me, when I ask what the consequences will be for the institution if the students, who are all on government scholarships, fail their tests. There must be some reasonable explanation for the disorganization, lack of attendance, lack of communication, and lack of consequences for students (or—for that matter—for faculty) who don't show up for class. Please, dear God, provide me with that insight before I lose all hope!

I ask myself for the umpteenth time why I am still here. But I have to admit that my many moments of frustration are balanced by those moments when I love the challenge, when I love the unpredictability of daily life, when I love the insights I am gaining into another culture (and into myself). I feel alive "living on the edge."

Tuesday, November 15

This is the fifth week of the semester. Again some new students trickle in. After about half an hour, Bagayogo comes into the room to tell me that the room we are in needs to be used for the graduate program and would we please move into the other building. The students and I traipse across the wide courtyard, up the many steps, only to find out that the room we have been sent to is occupied by the French teacher. We again end up in the media center, without any board to write on, and the students sitting so far apart that it is difficult for us to hear each other. A couple of students show up only minutes before the end of class and have the gall to ask me to mark them as present for the class on the enrollment register....

* * *

This evening I also started to teach my advanced conversation course at the Centre d'Etude et de Culture pour Jeunes (CECJ). The Center, together with its library and course offerings is managed by a Catholic nun, Sister Rosalie. What incredible difference from the chaos at the institute! Clean classroom, blackboard freshly wiped, a supply of chalk and a sponge! I even receive a bottle of water to keep my vocal cords hydrated in the hot air which seems to get dryer and dustier every day.

The class begins on time at 6 p.m. with 21 students, all Malian professionals or university students who pay to improve their English language skills and come to evening class after a day of work. The only thing I find perturbing is that 20 of the 21 students are male—a reminder of the dismal state of educational opportunities for women. But they appear to be very motivated and we have an interesting conversation about cultural differences.

* * *

I realize that generalizations about a culture are just that—generalizations which may not even apply to the majority of a group of people united by political boundaries, ethnicity, race, religion or other cultural variables. But the differences between American and Malian attitudes and lifestyles are striking. I sorely miss American individualism contrasted with the emphasis in Mali on family and clan. I miss the American "can-do attitude" and emphasis on problem solving, the "let's start right now," vs. the Malian *"insha Allah"* approach. I also miss the direct approach of dealing with issues, rather than the indirect Malian approach which often favors the solution of problems through intermediaries. Critical thinking and analysis as well as efficient organization are not yet the strengths of many people I deal with. But then, in the States as well, there too are masses of people who unquestioningly and uncritically accept religious or political dogma, not to mention the acceptance of whatever is new in pop culture or fashion. Superstitions, also, in the U.S. are generally somewhat more benign than in Mali. For instance, in the States I had not come across people who believed that intercourse with a virgin cured AIDS!

Back in Tubaniso

Wednesday, November 16

I GET UP at 5 a.m. and take a taxi to the Peace Corps office for the 7:15 a.m. shuttle to Tubaniso to join my young colleagues for in-service training for the rest of the week. In the afternoon, I lead a session, with the convoluted title: "Suggestions for Teacher Development in Formal Educational Settings or: What to look for when observing a class and how to (possibly...) change pedagogical practice." I had been told to prepare for a two-hour session but am interrupted after 90 minutes to make room on the program for a report of another volunteer. Why had I not been informed of the change in time allotment earlier?

Most of the remaining in-service training sessions are geared to my young colleagues who live in the bush rather than in the national capital. But I nevertheless find the sessions on making mud stoves, establishing literacy centers, preventing HIV/AIDS, improving nutrition, avoiding snake bites or creating educational opportunities especially for girls stimulating.

Tubaniso: I still can't aim my bodily excretions into the small round hole of the *njegen*; I still dislike the crowded mess of living with two others in a small mud hut. The added "attraction" this time of year is that one needs a blanket at night and the water for the morning shower is quite cold. But at least it no longer rains, and the pot holes through which I stumble on my way to and from the *refectoire* at night are now dry rather than filled with mud.

Saturday, November 19

Since I have teaching obligations on Monday and need to invent some instructional materials, I leave Tubaniso by Peace Corps van on Saturday evening to return to my apartment in Bamako. My young colleagues also plan to go to Bamako for some night life, but they will return to Tubaniso.

Open, Sesame!
Episode #1 Sunday, November 20

IT IS SUNDAY, but since I don't have access to a functioning computer at my apartment, I spend most of the day at the Peace Corps office. I get home after dark, but when I try to open my apartment door, the key neither turns nor can it be removed from the lock.

Two young women who appear to be the maids in the neighboring apartment try to help. No success! I call on a

Malian neighbor from downstairs. He also is unable to help. I call on a Cuban instructor who lives below, but he, too, is unsuccessful. I telephone Peace Corps security and am told to take a taxi to the Peace Corps rest house and try to find a bed there for the night—provided there is a free bed, and I am let in without having reservations—and to return to my locked abode first thing in the morning.

But I don't want to abandon my apartment with the key in the door; I don't want to miss classes the next morning; I don't want to spend another half hour and $6 to get back to Peace Corps to uncertain accommodations. My urge is to find lodging at the Radisson, but that, also, entails a taxi ride and furthermore, I would have to blow my entire monthly allowance on eight hours of clean sheets, air conditioning, and hot water. So I call Bagayogo for help. He reminds me—as if I did not know—that today is Sunday and no one at the institute is working. But wonders will never cease! He calls back after fifteen minutes to tell me that Moussa will be coming to fix the lock.

I wait. And I wait. The neighbor girl brings me a chair to sit outside my door. Thanks to Allah, there is a working light outside my door, but the mosquitoes and other biting bugs are fierce.

Moussa and his helper arrive on a *moto* after about an hour. They too can't get the Chinese piece of crap to relinquish the key. Finally, they use a hammer to knock out the lock. But by now it is 10 p.m. and the noise is awful. Neighbors come out of their apartments with wide-awake children in their arms, looking for the source of the noise. Finally the lock yields, but the door is so bent that Moussa cannot install a new lock. He leaves me with an open door and a promise to come back the next day for the necessary repairs. I no longer give a damn about my safety. I go under my mosquito net and sleep soundly.

Monday, November 21

I ask the neighbors to keep an eye on my apartment while I go to work.

To my amazement, the assistant to Bagayogo, shows up around 8:30 for roll call. My letter and many complaints about late arriving or non-attending students must have had some effect. However, for some reason my 10 o'clock students show up only around 11 a.m.

* * *

Moussa and his helper return to my apartment in the afternoon—as does Sali, my washer woman and dust remover (or rather, dust-distributor…).

The two men remove the bent steel door to be taken to some place where it can be straightened and a new lock installed. By 5 p.m.—again after lots of hammering—I can finally lock up my apartment again. I take a taxi to the *Tubab* store (Lebanese supermarket) and buy two bags of cookies: cheap Christmas cookies imported from Germany to be sold at unreasonable prices in Mali! These I present to the two immediate next door neighbors whose children were kept awake last night because of my door problem. I am sure that the remaining 24 families were also kept awake, but my Peace Corps allowance does not provide for such generosity.

Corruption

Tuesday, November 22

AFTER CLASSES, HILLARY, my Fulbright colleague at the institute, accompanies me home to admire the new lock and to share some left-over chili. In the afternoon, Amadou, my floor cleaner comes to wash the floors. The amount of dust that collects on floors and furniture (and dishes and food, etc.) through the open (glass-less) windows and doors in a couple of days here is absolutely amazing!

* * *

The evening conversation course at CECJ is again a delight. The topic (chosen by students) is "Corruption in Mali." The man who has prepared a presentation on the topic does not accept the theory that poverty or low wages are the main reasons for the prevailing corruption in all sectors of Malian culture. Rather, he believes that corruption is "in the blood" of Malians and "absorbed with their mother's milk." He cites the example of children accompanying their parents when these, successfully, bribe the teacher or principal to change their children's grades so that they can get promoted to the next grade. He himself is a teacher and he sees no solution to the problem of corruption.

Thanks to Allah, several students are less pessimistic. They express the view that corrupt practices can be changed, and that economic development in Mali—without a reduction of the level of corruption—is difficult if not impossible.

One student offers the opinion that there is no corruption in the United States because there is no poverty. He is surprised when I respond that there is poverty as well as corruption. I explain that laws and their enforcement, the demand for transparency by the system, as well as a free press have made corruption less rampant than in the developing world. Unfortunately, I have no optimistic prognosis for the poverty in the U.S.

Wednesday, November 23

The French director of the graduate program in arts management at the institute who lives and works in Paris, but comes to Mali several times a year to direct the program together with a Malian colleague (also working in Paris), has asked me to prepare a diagnostic English exam for entering students.

Unfortunately, only four of the ten newly admitted students (all working adults between 40 and 50 years of age) show up at the scheduled time, and my initial impression—verified by results of the exam—is that we need to start "at the beginning," though all of them have studied some English previously. Classes for the first and second year of the graduate program will begin in January.

In the afternoon—while on the computer at the Peace Corps office—I receive a message from the Peace

Corps Director, that he has approved my two nominations for a Summer Seminar on Social Entrepreneurship for Student Leaders in Developing Countries (funded by the U.S. Department of State) to go forward to the U.S. Embassy. The two students from the CECJ English Language Club, Mariam and Fouseyni, whom I had proposed for the program will be invited to formally apply and I need to help them with their application. I am delighted! Unfortunately, the deadline is already the following Monday and I am limited on what I can do, since I need to return to Tubaniso and am without access to the internet and to a computer.

Thanksgiving

Thursday, November 24

I HAVE RETURNED to Tubaniso for Thanksgiving and the last three days of in-service training for our remaining group of 20 volunteers. During my absence, the homologues of my colleagues have arrived for joint training. Since I don't have a homologue like the others, I tag along to the sessions which—to some extent—are already conducted in Bambara without translation. I admire the Bambara language skills acquired by my colleagues in just three short months and regret that I lack the competence to follow the presentations by various Malian presenters.

Thanksgiving is not a holiday in Mali, so classes only end in late afternoon. But my young colleagues frequently leave the sessions to accept cell phone Thanksgiving wishes from family and friends in the States.

By mid-afternoon I find out that some of my colleagues have received an "emergency message" on their cell phones that there has been another terrorist attack in the North of Mali, with four Europeans kidnapped. In case the story makes U.S. news, I call my daughter in Florida and assure her that I am fine.

My colleagues have decorated the *refectoire* (dining hall) for the holiday with handmade banners and plastic decorations sent by American mothers who miss their offspring.... The kitchen staff at Tubaniso, together with a number of "old" volunteers have prepared a Thanksgiving miracle with turkey (too little), chicken (too little), mashed potatoes, green beans, gravy, stuffing (from packages donated by volunteers who received Thanksgiving care-packages from home), as well as PUMPKIN PIE with ice cream rather than whipped cream.

A newly arrived group of forty Peace Corps trainees are permitted to leave their villages to join us for the Thanksgiving meal at Tubaniso. They, my colleagues, their homologues, as well as Peace Corps staff—about 100 people in all—greatly enjoy the American tradition of gorging yourselves in memory of the Pilgrim settlers, at a place thousands of miles away and almost 400 years ago.

Friday, November 25

Another terrorist attack! And this one for the first time south of the river Niger: Three kidnapped, one shot— in a restaurant during bright daylight! One woman escaped. Some of my colleagues fear that Peace Corps will be evacuated for security reasons. U.S. Marines are in Gao to help train the Malian Army to deal with terrorists. I wish them good luck in the vast stretches of the sparsely inhabited areas of the Saharan desert!

Saturday, November 26

The American Director of Peace Corps Mali comes to Tubaniso to reassure us. Mali is a large country and, so far, all attacks have been in the north, 240 km from the nearest volunteer station in Mali, and off-limits to us for travel since the first kidnapping incident. He does, however, express concern that these attacks have now moved south of the Niger. While Dogon Country, where a number of my young colleagues plan to spend the Christmas holidays, is not yet forbidden to us, we are discouraged to travel there, particularly in large groups.

I return to Bamako by Peace Corps van in the evening. My colleagues will return to their stations the following days.

How to become rich and famous

Sunday, November 27

MARIAM AND FOUSEYNI, the two students I nominated for the State Department scholarship, spend the morning at my apartment working on their applications for the scholarship. I am impressed by Mariam's perceptive intelligence, evident in her draft statement of why she "should be selected for the scholarship in the United States." However, it takes some time to explain to Fouseyni why the U.S. taxpayer may not want to fund him because he wants "to become rich and famous and an important businessman," but rather for what he wants to do for his fellow citizens.

Since I will not have access to a computer to look over their final submissions before the deadline, I send them home with an *insha Allah*!

It would be fantastic if these two young people could experience first hand, by American example, that bribes and "gifts," large family size, polygamy, forced or child marriages, child labor, bride price, gender discrimination in education, business and politics, female genital mutilation, and reliance on external funding and expertise rather than self initiative may hinder rather than help economic and social development. Without my prompting, Mariam has cited JFK in her statement, writing "Don't ask what your country can do for you, but ask what you can do for your country." That a girl!

Good help is hard to get

Tuesday, November 29

BAGAYOGO CALLED YESTERDAY (don't ask me why he can't delegate this type of work....) to tell me that third year classes were cancelled for today. I am staying home, expecting Salah from Peace Corps maintenance to come and finally repair my chairs before they totally collapse, as well as some other odds and ends which I had unsuccessfully tried to get repaired with the help of the institute. Salah arrives with the Education Program Manager to make an inventory of everything that should be done.

They depart and later return with a carpenter, and finally leave me with the carpenter to start the repair projects. The carpenter has to interrupt his work a number of times because he lacks a certain tool, and by the end of the afternoon has not got very far. He promises to return on Wednesday.

* * *

For the evening course at CECJ, this time the topic selected by one of the course participants is "Good and dangerous Malian customs." The positive customs described by the student leading the discussion are the extended family and *cousinage* systems, and the informal money saving and lending system (called *tontine*) which depend totally on trust.

As dangerous customs he lists female genital mutilation (FGM) and forced marriage. The majority of his classmates appear to share his opinions. Two disagree openly. One male whom I estimate to be in his late 30s or early 40s passionately supports FMG, because "it has been tradition for hundreds of years! It helps women remain faithful! And women are not hurt by it." (!) The only female student in class—a university student in her 20s—is in favor of arranged marriage because "my parents know the family of the intended husband. They know best what is good for me."

I am again experiencing that unsettling shock, where one minute I feel totally at ease interacting with educated Malians as my equals, in the context of what I perceive to be a shared human experience and similar aspirations, only to be suddenly confronted by something said or seen which reminds me that I am living in alien territory and that my opinions, perceptions, and cultural expectations are very different from many in my host country.

My initial urge is to hold forth and lecture on the evils of FGM as well as forced marriage or child marriage, but I remember instruction during Peace Corps training that as development workers we should not try to impose our own opinions and value systems on the host culture, but rather provide information and encouragement to help change those aspects of traditional culture which infringe on human rights or development.

So, in response to the opinion expressed that women are not hurt by FGM, I just tell of my experience of visiting a center for women suffering from FGM-related physical (and mental) damage in Mopti. There I encountered teen-age women without bladder control who had been abandoned or divorced by their husbands; women with irreparably damaged cervixes during child birth due to FGM; women with constant urinary tract infections because anal and urinary tracts were no longer separate, etc.

I feel reassured when one of the classmates tells the spokesman who is in favor of FGM that he would not need to travel to far-away Mopti to witness possible after-effects of FGM, but that one of these centers supporting women suffering from FGM-related injuries could be found in a neighboring town. There is hope!

All that jazz. . . .

Wednesday, November 30

THE CARPENTER RETURNS to continue the repair jobs in my apartment. Again, he does not have all necessary parts and tools, and again he leaves with the work uncompleted and a promise to call me when he is ready to finish the job. I am certainly glad that I don't have to pay him by the hour.

This evening the U.S. Embassy—in the context of its cultural exchange program—is sponsoring a concert by the Ari Roland Jazz Quartet at the Patio in the French Cultural Center. I sit with Hillary, my Fulbright colleague at the institute who will be the featured singer tonight, the musicians (when they are not playing), and some Embassy employees. The base player (Ari Roland), drummer (Keith Balla) and two saxophone players (Chris Byars and Zaid Nasser) are excellent jazz musicians. It almost feels like home at a concert of the Tucson Jazz Society.

Friday, December 2

The Ari Roland Jazz Quartet is to come to the art institute to give a workshop for the music students and hold a jam session afterwards. Even though I am not teaching today, I go along to watch and listen. Only three of the musicians arrive. The fourth is in bed at the hotel with a Malian "bug" and 104 degrees fever.

I am delighted to notice the interest and motivation

of the students participating in the workshop. Spirits are high, and the event is a great success. Even Africable (West African TV Cable company) is present in full force to record the happenings. I may be on TV tonight!

I also finally get to meet the co-director of the graduate program. Unfortunately, we don't have much time to talk, since he will be leaving for Paris this evening. But he promises to contact me upon his return in January to discuss his expectations of and recommendations for what I am to do with the group.

Saturday, December 3

The German Embassy is sponsoring a *Weihnachtsmarkt* (Christmas market) at the Palais de Culture with vendors of traditional Malian and not-so-traditional arts and crafts, food booths, and cultural performances. The Ari Roland Jazz Quartet—together with Hillary—is one of the performing groups, compliments of the American Embassy and my tax dollars. Seeing the positive reaction of the spectators and the positive visibility for my country provided through these artists convinces me that my tax dollars are well spent.

The setting is great: beautiful, high-quality crafts (although expensive); some quasi-German Christmas goodies; and traders only half as aggressive as in downtown Bamako. There is, however, little that reminds one of German (or American) holiday traditions, except a Christmas tree made of beer cans....

At departure, I am proud that I had spent no money at the Christmas fair. However, just as I am leaving, one of the traders talks me into buying a Benin bronze at a price I cannot possible refuse, even if I have to go again into my social security check to supplement my Peace Corps living allowance.

In the evening I attend the last concert by the Ari Roland Jazz Quartet, this one co-sponsored by the U.S. Embassy with some NGO in the National Park. Nice experience, though the chairs only fill up an hour after the concert's supposed starting time. The second part of the concert is played by a Malian group of musicians. The rhythm is great, but, as usual, I have difficulties getting into the monotony and repetitiveness of traditional Malian music. However, the young Malians—dressed to the gills—obviously don't share my difficulties and dance enthusiastically to the tunes.

As the evening progresses, it is getting quite cool. Both Hillary and I are shivering when we leave the park around 11 p.m. to find a taxi to our respective residences.

Midterm

Monday, December 5

THIS IS WEEK number eight at the art institute and I am giving mid-term exams to both classes I teach on Mondays. In spite of my introductory speech discouraging cheating, attempts at cheating are rampant! In spite of postponing the beginning of the exam for half an hour, several students arrive late and have to go in search of chairs to sit on. The electricity does not work in the room and it is so dark that I can hardly recognize the black faces in front of me.

Tuesday, December 6

I am planning to give the midterm to the multi-media and plastic arts majors I teach on Tuesdays. I assume we will be in the media center again and I go to re-arrange tables and chairs in the center so students don't sit on top of each other. The blackboard that was in the room the week before has vanished. I sent one of the workers to try to find a board, but his French is incomprehensible and for some reason he can't do it. It is past 8:15, but no students have yet arrived. I wait. I go outside the center and inquire among the students sitting around where the third-year students are. They don't know. At 9:30 a.m. still no students. I go see Bagayogo who tells me that the third-year students have a workshop today and that he forgot to notify me. Luckily, I don't have to sit around until 12:30 to wait for the van back to the apartments. Bagayogo and the chair of the music department need to go into Bamako and take me back home.

In the afternoon I am meeting with Mr. Coulibaly, the President of the Malian Association of Teachers of English (MATE). MATE is apparently non-functional, and the American Embassy has encouraged me to become involved and see whether I can help to reenergize the group. Coulibaly wanted to meet at the U.S. Embassy, but since I dislike the searches and complicated security procedures, as well as the time it takes to get permission to enter the inner sanctum there, I suggested that we meet instead at the CECJ before my evening class.

Coulibaly received an M.A. from an American university in the 1990s. He regrets several times during our conversation that he is not computer literate. I find it hard to believe that he was able to get an American degree, and that he can now work as English professor at the university without being able to use a computer. According to him, the association's problems are due to political infighting and lack of commitment by members of the board. We agree that I should attend the next meeting of the association.

* * *

In the evening I am meeting again with my advanced conversation students at CECJ and today's topic is "marriage." There are two discussion leaders, the sole female student and the advocate of FGM—both probably the two most conservative members of the class. They advocate the traditional Moslem party line of arranged marriage, polygamy, and large families. The remaining students—I don't know whether out of conviction or whether to please me—seem to be open to more western ideas of matrimony.

I make them aware that polygamy, early (arranged or forced) marriages, and lack of women's education contribute to the huge birth rate in Mali (6.4 children per woman), and the 3.1% annual increase in population, which is predicted to lead to a doubling of the population within twenty years. We discuss the effect of such a population growth on available resources (e.g., water, food, education, medical care, housing, availability of jobs, availability of wood for cooking fuel, etc.), on the environment, and on the standard of living. Mali is drowning in garbage now with 13 Million people. What will happen with 26 Million? Deforestation is contributing to soil erosion and desertification now. What will happen with double that population?

It is obvious, that many of these educated adults have never thought of the effects of population growth on development. Some obviously see the light! Some blame all of Mali's present and future problems on the French, their past colonial masters. Some see all solutions in the hands of external support and foreign NGOs. All overestimate Mali's available resources, a country that is two thirds desert. The little gold that is mined in the western part of the country and the salt mines in the Sahara don't contribute much to the national tax coffers. Neither does the export of cotton, peanuts and other agricultural products.

* * *

IN ONE WEEK I WILL BE LEAVING FOR THE STATES TO CHECK OUT MY HOUSE AND VISIT WITH FRIENDS IN TUCSON, AND THEN SPEND CHRISTMAS WITH MY GRANDCHILDREN IN ST. PETERSBURG. I CAN'T WAIT!

Reverse culture shock

Sunday, January 15, 2012

I HAVE BEEN back in Bamako for two weeks now and this is the first time I get around to write into my journal since my departure for the U.S. on December 13.

My visit back to "God's country" was just what I needed to recharge my batteries. My friend Al was waiting for me at the airport with roses and a working cell phone; Rachel, Mary and Elfriede had seen to it that my house was in tip top shape, and that the refrigerator was stocked with survival food; there were even some Christmas decorations! The only problems encountered were an empty car battery, and that I had selected days with near freezing temperatures for my visit.

It was damn cold in the house and I had no hot water, since I had had the gas disconnected before I left for the Peace Corps. I decided to have the gas reconnected for my short stay in Tucson, but was told that the gas company needed five days notice to do the job. In Mali I could have bribed my way into getting the requested service immediately, but I remembered vaguely that slipping a twenty-dollar bill to the company rep at the counter was not the American way -☺ Thanks to Allah I had some training in taking bucket baths, and the fire place served passably as central heating unit.

My short time in Tucson was filled with one party after the other, and I was quite overwhelmed by the interest, affection and concern shown me by all of my friends.

While in Mali, I had contacted the Center for English as a Second Language (CESL) at the University of Arizona for some help obtaining instructional materials, and a former student of mine, together with CESL's librarian, saw to it that a whole lot of books and CDs were waiting for me to be picked up and shipped to Mali, as I get the necessary funds to cover the expensive mailing cost. This will be a major help, since students have no textbooks, and everything I had gleaned from the internet and prepared in advance for instruction was lost when my computer was stolen.

In spite of having been in Mali for just seven months, I suffered from some re-entry shock into the U.S. Some of my "new" impressions were positive, some negative. What an amazingly clean, orderly, and organized place Americans live in! How disciplined the drivers are! There are no hordes of motor scooters whipping in and out between cars and *sotramas*. There are no taxis with broken windshields or loose-hanging doors. There are working street lights! There are no open sewers, and few uneven pavements to stumble on. One can sit around the house in the evening without using a gallon of mosquito repellent. And I could leave food out on the kitchen counter for more than three minutes without it attracting immediately an army of ants, flies, and other vermin.

At least to the observer coming from Sub-Saharan Africa, there is an appearance of overwhelming prosperity, an over-choice of products in all categories; and compared with Mali, the prices are quite inexpensive. While drooling over the inventory at Trader Joe's, I noticed that many items cost only one fourth the price charged in Bamako.

But after the first euphoria of being back in "God's country," I noted some negative aspects of my culture. I realized that for the first time in seven months I am constantly put on hold when using the phone. For the first time in seven months I have to deal with an automatic voice that directs me via umpteen options to another automatic voice which invariably does not provide the answer to my need. I went to war with my cable company which was still deducting monthly payments from my bank account in spite of my cancelation of the service last May, and despite several lengthy e-mails sent from Mali. Since neither my e-mails nor my phone calls worked to get me disconnected, I finally drove to the company's physical plant and threatened the woman staffing the counter with a sit-in. I was promised a refund, but a couple of days after my return to Mali I received another bill....

I also noted the many homeless people and pan handlers. In Mali, apart from the number of children who attend Koranic schools and beg for food, the largest group of beggars one encounters are the blind or otherwise physically challenged. In Tucson most of those begging looked perfectly able bodied.

I was getting upset by the constant inundation with advertising, the constant urge to consume: "If you respond in the next 60 minutes, you will only pay $9.99 and, in fact, we will send you two widgets instead of one...."

And after re-entering the U.S. political fray on television, I have to agree with Michael Sandel, that we have moved from a market economy to a market society: Not just consumer goods, but everything in public life appears to be available for purchase. Those who have money can buy opportunities, justice, recognition, influence, political elections and a place on the ballot. Those without money definitely lack "equality" in most aspects of life. American democracy means no longer "We the people...," but "We, the people with money...."

I am not sure whether I prefer the impersonal interaction when shopping or doing other business in the U.S. to the friendly bantering when doing business in Mali.

I missed the little *butigi* right around the corner where I can get the necessities of life without putting on make-up and starting the car.

And I missed the solicitousness of Malians toward older people. No American children came running to help me carry my grocery bags. No one helped me get off the bus. No one grabbed my hand to lead me through traffic.

On December 23 I locked up my Tucson home and flew to Florida to spend Christmas and a great week with my daughter and family in St. Petersburg. My son-in-law was waiting for me with a new computer to replace the one stolen in Mali. I was delighted to note that my 12-year old granddaughter actually seemed to enjoy spending time with me. My grandson, unfortunately, still prefers the TV and electronic games. . . . Both have become accomplished skate boarders and own enough of those contraptions to equip a national team.

My granddaughter baked chocolate chip cookies, and my son-in law fixed duck for Christmas dinner which probably account for three of the five pounds I gained during my two-week stay in the States.

I experienced additional "reverse culture shock" comparing the number of toys owned by my grandchildren with those of the children in my Bamako neighborhood. The cost of my grandchildren's Christmas gifts probably constituted the annual income of a Malian laborer.

My daughter took me along to the lovely Don Cesar, a luxury resort on the Gulf of Mexico where she works as physical trainer and teaches exercise classes to people who have probably never wondered where the next day's food will come from or how to pay for the medical treatment of a sick child.

I spent New Year's Eve on Delta Airlines over the Atlantic Ocean on my return trip to Bamako via Paris, a long, tiring, but otherwise uneventful trip.

Back in "Allah's country"

I ARRIVED AT my apartment on January 1, shortly before midnight local time. The taxi driver lugged my two suitcases of 50 lbs. each the 44 steps to my door. Nothing in my apartment was missing, but everything was covered by a layer of sand and dust. I decided to excavate the place the next day and called it a day on a fresh sheet, but under an incredibly dusty mosquito net.

* * *

Before leaving Mali I had been told that classes would resume on January 2. Awfully jet-lagged, I had enough sense to call before taking off for my teaching duties early in the morning and was told that classes would only begin on January 3.

* * *

Somehow I had subconsciously expected that the administration of my major place of work would miraculously become efficient during the Christmas break, that the totally overburdened assistant director would have learned to delegate some of the menial duties, that the classrooms would be cleaned before the beginning of classes (I regularly encounter the women who sweep or wash the floors of the premises way after classes are scheduled to begin), that courses would start on time, that a majority of students would actually show up, and that there would be clean chairs and a usable blackboard. No such luck! Instead, the lights did not work in the classroom I was supposed to teach in, and I ended up again teaching in the media center. There was not much English learning going on, but the Hershey's chocolate kisses and mini candy bars that I brought along for my students from the States were greatly appreciated!

How not to run a language fair

I ALSO STARTED teaching a new course at the CECJ, and the CECJ English Club was moving into high gear in preparation of the English language competition that was scheduled to take place on January 14.

The Club had several extraordinary planning meetings for the language competition during last week, one of them at my apartment. Things got a little rowdy with ten people in my living room, but we were productive and my fellow Club members ate everything in the apartment that I could find.

Already in October the English Club had submitted a proposal for funding of the language competition to the U.S. Embassy. Embassy staff finally met with the Club on January 4, but they had, unfortunately, not remembered that the event was to take place already the following week. They did, however, sound positive and promised to respond very soon. In fact, the Embassy staff indicated that someone from their office might be in attendance for the competition. All of the Club members, including myself and Sister Rosalie, the Director of CECJ, were very optimistic that some financial assistance for the event would be forthcoming.

But by Thursday we still had not heard from the Embassy—despite an e-mail reminder that I had sent the preceding Sunday. However, we all were so sure we would get some support—at least in the form of a few dictionaries for prizes—that we officially acknowledged "the US

Embassy's contribution" on what was to be the final copy of the program for the language competition.

It goes without saying, that I was embarrassed by the lack of response from the representatives of my government and did not quite know how to explain it. All that it would have taken was "sorry, but we don't have any money for this." (In retrospect, prioritizing the rising unrest in the north of the country with the needs of the English Language Club may have been problematic for embassy personnel ....)

Fourteen hours before the competition was to start, we still did not know exactly where the prizes for the winners of the various competitions were to come from. Thanks be to Allah, the All Knowing and All Merciful, friends back in Tucson had funded the mailing of some of the books donated by CESL which had arrived and they, in addition to some books contributed by CECJ, some English dictionaries we bought, together with cheap back packs, could be assembled to be used as prizes the following day.

* * *

And then, yesterday, Saturday, January 14, was the big day! When I arrived at CECJ at 7 a.m., a number of the contest participants were already waiting, and things started to get chaotic before the competition even started. By 8:30 there were over 100 eager students grades seven to nine and their teachers from nine area junior high schools. Initially, ten schools were to participate, but one school cancelled because the teachers were on strike.

The person in charge of student registration came late

and things became more chaotic yet! There was an electricity outage and the technician (who also came late) had problems connecting the microphone.

The event started with a "knowledge competition" with questions in four categories: history, geography, language/ grammar, and important persons. Three students from each school (a total of 27) sat on a make-shift podium and answered general knowledge questions. At 9 a.m. we were already half hour behind schedule, mainly because the TV station was present and the crew insisted that—before their departure to another job—we interrupt the contest and simulate an award ceremony for the evening news. I advised against such a simulated first prize award, as I could just imagine the reaction of American parents watching the evening news, finding out that their offspring had won first prize, only to be told later that this was not really true. My advice was not heeded!

When preparing the questions for the knowledge competition, we had not anticipated so many ties between the competing teams. So, we ran out of questions in the history category during the third round.

When it came time for refreshments (pop corn, peanuts, bananas and soft drinks) we were one hour late.

The next event in the contest was to be a "conversation test." I had made arrangements for six Peace Corps Volunteers to serve as "raters" for the oral interview and they, together with six Malian members of the English Club, met with individual students in each of the three grades for short question/answer sessions on topics such as "my school," "my family," "a trip I took," etc.

To save time, we divided the students into six groups (major chaos!) and conducted the interviews in six classrooms. Originally, the Americans were to ask the questions for the short interviews, but Club members then decided that the students would not be able to understand native speakers of English, and that they (i.e., only the Maliens) should do the talking during the tests—though several are themselves hard to understand when speaking English. As ridiculous as this sounds, it probably was a wise decision to have the Malians do the talking in English, since I found out during the event that practically none of the grade 7-9 students understood what I said, although my English is generally more comprehensible than that of native-born sons or daughters of Texas or Alabama. . . .

It would take a word with a stronger meaning than "chaotic" to describe what actually went on. Although I had insisted that we rehearse the procedures the day before, no one took the initiative to implement them.

The final event was a spelling contest. Club members had decided to replicate a spelling bee, as shown in the film "Akeelah and the Bee" which I had shown at one of the club meetings. Unfortunately, I was occupied collecting the results of the conversation test and was not present at the beginning of the spelling bee. Somehow, instead of following the planned procedure and using two students per grade per school (i.e., about 60 students), they opted to open the spelling competition to volunteers. In short, the spelling bee appeared to be endless and the troops got really restless.

Amazingly, the contest ended only 75 minutes late

with much cheering and enthusiasm during the announce-
ment of the winners and the awarding of prizes, followed
by many photo opportunities. I was a wreck, but English
Club members were satisfied and thought the competition
was a great success. I guess it is all about what you are used
to....

Adjusted?

Sunday, January 16

THE NIGHTS ARE deliciously cool at present. I am even
using the Mexican cotton blanket that my predecessor,
Jeremy, left behind at his departure from Mali.

I have my first dinner guests today: Hillary comes with
a visiting friend who is about my age and who teaches ethnomusicology in a South African university. Helen, the
visitor, is appalled by my neighborhood. She comments
on the families living in garages a few yards from the
apartments, the garbage heap across the yard, the dust
and the dirt, the laundry hanging over the walls all over,
the occasional goat meandering about, the dilapidated
furniture in my apartment and the walls that are in dire
need of a coat of paint.

I note for the first time that I am no longer aware
of the conditions of my surroundings. I guess this means
that I have adjusted! In fact, when I first arrived and
everything was "new," "different," and "strange," I took
photos galore (all lost now with my stolen camera). Now I
no longer notice what formerly constituted photo opportunities, and I have not yet taken one picture with the

new camera I brought back from the States. We marvel at the human ability to adjust to practically any condition, an ability we probably developed as a technique for self-preservation. If we wouldn't, we'd go nuts or die!

End-of-semester chaos

January 17

TODAY WAS MY last teaching day of the semester. Final exams will begin next week. I have survived my first semester at the institute, but still do not have a regular classroom. I continue to teach in the media center, with people coming in and out, loud conversations in the background, low student attendance, and each time a hassle to get a portable blackboard. Sometimes people not enrolled in the course—including some of the Cuban faculty—sit among the regular students as well.

Just to check whether my perceptions jive with reality, I calculated the student attendance rate for my classes. Here they are: Music students—attendance rate during the semester about 48%; Plastic Arts students—attendance rate 56%; Theater and Multi-Media students—about 62%.

This does not take into account that many students come very late to class and that—categorically—no class begins on time.

* * *

There appears to be no schedule for the final exams. I am told that I can determine my own times for semester finals. I select the regular class times, hoping for the least confusion. But the students from my 10 o-clock course tell me that another professor has already taken that time for next week. . . . Will I ever understand "the system," or how it works? Or will I learn how to function in an academic context without a system, without getting stressed out?

* * *

Apparently there are no rules against sexual harassment in Cuba. One of the older Cuban males who arrived in November and teaches guitar first started to move on me; but then he decided that I was either too old or too non-receptive to his pawing and compliments, and he moved on to my younger Fulbright colleague, Hillary. Hillary tells me that he is absolutely obnoxious. Today he came into her class while she was teaching, babbling in Spanish (he practically speaks no French) and making loud compliments in broken English. He is not discouraged by her obvious hostility. She thinks he has a mental problem.

* * *

I have no idea how the Cubans are teaching, since many—particularly the newcomers among them—have little, if any French competence. Even considering that most of them teach the performing arts (e.g., dance or musical instruments), and the plastic arts (painting and sculpture), one would assume that being able to communicate in a common language would greatly improve instruction and learning.

In retrospect, given my experience with Malian education, I am gaining increased respect for my former African students at the University of Arizona. I cannot even imagine the "culture shock" they experienced when transferring from the chaos and disorganization here to the American system of higher education. There were, for instance, Itangaza (Congo Kinsasha) who still counts among the brightest doctoral students I have had; and there was Hassan (Sudan) who tried valiantly to stay awake in one of my early evening classes during the Ramadan fast.

A paint job

Friday, Saturday and half of Sunday, January 20, 21, and 22

WHEN MOVING TO Medina Coura I had been told by the institute's administrators that my apartment could be painted. After requesting dozens of times that this be done, Brehima, one of the cleaning crew at the institute, finally comes to do the job. He speaks very little French and communication is extremely difficult. I am made to understand that the institute has supplied the paint and I am to pay for the labor. He comes with one paint roller and does a fair job without a ladder, without masking tape, without a scraper. To make the job easier, I let him use the same yellow that originally covered the walls.

Brehima charges me 10,000 CFA (approximately $20)

for the paint job, plus another 5,000 CFA for additional paint needed, since the institute is closed on week ends. I know that the Cubans only paid him half that amount to have their units painted. I do, however, not insist on being treated equally, since giving him anything less than what he asked for would be sheer exploitation. And, of course, Americans are known to be richer than Cubans....

Chaos continues

Monday, January 23

I AM SO angry I could scream!

The van is 30 minutes late for the transportation to school. I arrive at the institute, ready to give exams. Some of my students are already waiting in the court yard, but make me aware that there may be scheduling problems. I find an exam schedule for Monday and Tuesday that had apparently been posted in the hall of the administration building late on Friday. Students mill around—as confused as I am. My courses are not listed. I climb the stairs to Bagayogo's office. As usual, he is multi-tasking, has excuses for the lack of communication, and has no idea what is going on. I show my irritation at not being informed of the changes and of the waste of my time.

My exams are being re-scheduled for Wednesday at 8 a.m. I wonder how the students will find out about that, but decide that this is no longer my problem. I ask for some additional copies of the exam to be made, but the copier does not work. I guess I will have to spend the time and money to go back to the Peace Corps office to use the copier there. How does one get across to Malians that time is a non-renewable resource?

Rather than wait for the 12:30 p.m. van to the apartment complex, I insist on being driven back early. I wonder whether I should ask the Peace Corps for a change in job placement. But the University of Bamako has been closed ever since I arrived in the country, and the Language Center of the Ministry of Education does not appear to be very interested in my services.

Trouble in River City

Thursday, February 2

MAN, OH MAN! This really is no place for the mentally fragile!

We volunteers have been bombarded for the past week with security alerts by the Embassy and the Peace Corps: muggings of volunteers and other *tubabus* in Bamako, prohibitions to travel to Dakar during the elections, five separate attacks by Tuaregs on Malian Army installations in the north with numerous casualties. Today the unrest arrived in Bamako.

As usual, I go downstairs at 7:45 a.m. to wait for the van to take me to the institute. I wait. And I wait. Strangely, none of my Cuban colleagues are joining me as usual in the wait for transportation. At 8:15 I call Lili, my former Cuban neighbor, to ask whether they will be going to work today. I cannot understand her response in its totality, but get that the Cubans have been told by their embassy to stay home today.

I call Bagayogo. He, too, is still at home and tells me that he will not be coming to campus today because of the unrest and potential violence downtown. He suggests that I also stay home. I go back to my apartment.

A little while later, I get an emergency phone message from Peace Corps Security, telling me to avoid downtown Bamako today. I call Hillary. She did go to the institute by taxi and the institute is not closed. She tells me that some of the students are there, but not enough to administer her final exam.

This is what I understand: The Malian government has sent several army divisions up north to help quell the Tuareg uprising. Numerous people have been killed and thousands have fled their homes, but President Touré apparently is willing to negotiate and has decreed that the soldiers not shoot back. The wives and husbands of the soldiers (there are female soldiers in the Malian military) have apparently not been told anything about their spouses' deployment, their whereabouts, safety or conditions. So today a group of women and children march on the presidential residence, and there are huge demonstrations downtown and in front of various ministries. From my balcony I see hundreds of mostly young men noisily streaming by.

The Tuareg—a still partially nomadic, Berber-related minority living all over the Sahel—have caused unrest in Mali before in the early 1990s, 2000 and 2006. But their demand for an independent state was rejected and they agreed to a cease-fire in exchange for government promises to distribute jobs, resources, and leadership opportunities more equitably among tribes.

It is a fact that Libya's Col. Qadhafi was a friend and financial supporter of Mali, and quite a number of Malians (mostly Tuaregs who consider themselves more Arab than Africans) fought for him before and during the Libyan revolution. They have now returned home, jobless, without money or employment possibilities. It is assumed that these returned Tuareg mercenary soldiers are the cause of the unrest and fighting in Northern Mali. Tribalism is clearly a if not THE major impediment to development and peace in Africa. The second impediment is religion!

Anyway, I stay home. Around 1 p.m. I get a call from one of the English Club members. She tells me that her little sister is attending a school near my apartment, but has been released from school early because of the demonstrations. She asks me whether the girl can come to my place and stay until it is safe to go home. Of course, I agree, and 14-year old Rosalie is now sleeping in her lovely light blue dress on my dusty living room couch.

* * *

I am sharing with Rosalie some of the banana bread I have baked. It has turned out somewhat hard (I can't control the oven temperature), but she obviously likes it. She carefully tears one of the paper napkins in half and returns the unused half to the stack I put before her. My grandson would have used half a dozen napkins for the occasion!

Rosalie's mother (an attractive woman about my daughter's age) picks up her daughter on her *moto* around 4 p.m. She tells me of vandalism and property damage observed on the way and warns me to stay home.

But an hour later I dare to go out anyway, hoping to copy some materials at the Peace Corps for tomorrow's class, provided that classes will resume. The taxi driver tells me that the demonstrators have gone home, but I see some make-shift barriers they constructed on the streets, a tumbled monument, and a still smoldering heap of tires. Most stores are closed. Only the market women along the streets have resumed their commerce in bananas, oranges, onions and Maggi boullion cubes.

The Peace Corps office is full of volunteers who have been stranded in town, unable to return to their work sites because of the unrest. We are advised by e-mail and SMSs to "stay in" for the evening.

Friday, February 3

The city appears to be calm, but the Peace Corps office is still closed. I take a taxi to the U.S. Embassy where I have a lunch date with the assistant public affairs officer. Security has been tightened. In addition to my phone, i-pod and flash drive, I have to leave behind my lipstick, sun screen and mosquito repellent before entering the inner sanctum. The Marines are in full battle dress. Because of anticipated continuing unrest, the Embassy also closes early.

As penance for not honoring their promise to support the English language fair a couple of weeks ago, I get the opportunity to select some books in an embassy storeroom for the libraries of both the institute and CECJ. Great! For lunch we go to "The Great Wall," an expensive, elegant Chinese restaurant with ornate table linens and a non-working toilet. We are the only guests. The food is great! On the way back we pass the Raddisson Hotel where a number of helmeted, battle-equipped police crowd on benches in the rear of an open truck. How reassuring to see that those who can afford to frequent the Raddisson are protected!

In the evening I attend a regular meeting of the English Club at CECJ. Tempers and discussion are heated, and the topic is, of course, the Tuareg rebellion up north, and President Amadou Toumani Touré's apparent unwillingness or inability to quell it by armed force. My young friends advocate for outright civil war! Some of them put forth conspiracy theories, blaming the unrest directly on A.T.T. (the President who is serving his second and constitutionally declared last term) who, according to them, "wants to stay in power and avoid the upcoming elections which cannot take place as long as there is regional unrest." Given recent history in Ivory Coast, the Congo, Senegal, Libya, Zimbabwe, etc. where political leaders have declared themselves (or at least tried to declare themselves) 'President for life' (to be followed in the job by one of their sons), this is not too far-fetched, but unlikely to happen in Mali. After all, we have been reassured on multiple occasions that Mali is a model among emerging democracies in West Africa.

Harmattan

February 7

LIFE APPEARS TO be back to "normal." However, now there is a weather warning from the U.S. Embassy, recommending that we stay inside and not exercise outdoors. The cold winds coming from the Sahara this time of year—called the Harmattan—are blowing in full force. It actually feels cold (it may be as low as 60 degrees during the night and mornings).

I am wearing the only jacket I brought along. People are bundled up, including turbans and face coverings or breathing masks for many *moto* drivers and pedestrians. Visibility is less than 100 meters. The blowing dust is incredible! Many people (including myself) have throat or breathing problems. Since my windows have no glass, the wind blows through the place and everything is covered by layers of dust and sand.

A Malian wedding

Sunday, February 12

WHEN BAGAYOGO HANDED me an invitation to his daughter's wedding earlier this week, I knew it would be a grandiose event, because the invitation was plasticized and listed 13 participating families (seven on the groom's side and six on the bride's). There was to be a civil ceremony at the town hall in Kati at 9 a.m. and a religious ceremony at the local mosque at 4 p.m.

Not knowing how to proceed (should I go? Should I bring a gift? What should I wear? etc.), I called Mohamed, my Bambara instructor and general consultant on things cultural. After consulting with his wife (like in the U.S., weddings are mostly women's business), he told me I should go; I should plan to attend the civil ceremony only; I would not need to bring a wedding gift, but if I insisted, I could bring a *pagne* (a piece of fabric to make a wrapper for the bride) or some sheets; and I should dress "formally."

Given my own cultural conditioning, a wedding gift should not (totally) ignore the husband, and furthermore, most Malian middle class women have enough *pagnes* to dress a girls' school. So I am looking for sheets. The quality of sheets at the market is pretty flimsy (made in China); at the import store they are too expensive (made in China), and anyway, I don't know what kind of bed the young couple will have. So, instead, I buy a water carafe and six tumblers (made in China, the English label on the package with spelling errors). Given my preference for Danish modern, this is not quite what I would have chosen for myself, but the female Malian security guard at the Peace Corps whom I consult finds my purchase absolutely beautiful.

Eight of my Cuban colleagues (roughly half of the group teaching at the institute) are also going and Guantanamo, the driver (I know him only by this nickname), picks us up a little after 8 a.m. for the 40-minute drive to Kati, a small town with a large military base where the Bagayogo family resides.

We are ushered through the many *motos* parked in the

entry way into the compound and seated on plastic lawn chairs and rented stackable steel chairs. Masses of ornately dressed people come and go, most of them enter the actual house, I assume to greet the predominantly female representatives of the various clan families.

The remains of food on the ground of the courtyard indicate that the dishes have been done there earlier this morning. Unfortunately, the flies have noticed this as well, and we constantly have to defend ourselves against their aggressive attacks.

After a little while and many introductions, a gentleman, dressed in a bright, blue and orange bazin outfit starts hollering loudly in Bambara at a man and his son who are sitting on the opposite side of the courtyard. He gets quite agitated, prancing back and forth, gesticulating wildly. In my opinion, this is one hell of a time to start a fight!

I ask the man sitting next to me why the guy is so angry. I am surprised to be told that the bazin-clad shouter is not angry at all. Rather, he is a *griot* and is extolling the accomplishments and family history of the man he is screaming at or about. I had heard about *griots;* in fact I had already experienced some. But they had always been singers (women or men) who flattered whoever paid them with songs of praise for themselves, their families, clan or ancestors. This one did not sing! For the 1,460th time I wish I had stuck with my Bambara instruction during Peace Corps training so that I could understand more than names and isolated words!

* * *

I wonder how cultural anthropologists who do not speak the local language arrive at their interpretations regarding the meaning of similar cultural rituals which are so different from our own. In the future, I will read Margaret Meade with a grain of salt—although I believe, she actually lived for a considerable time with the Pacific Islanders whose culture she described.

* * *

No written description can do justice to the female wedding guests: their colorfully embroidered attire (each outfit different), glittering jewelry, elaborate hairdos, wigs or head dresses, carefully applied henna design on hands and feet, artistically decorated nails, kohled eyes, erased eyebrows, and more or less tastefully applied make-up have to be seen to be believed! I think half of Mali's GNP for 2012 was spent on the outfits for this event! To spend beyond your means for a wedding is apparently not just an American cultural tradition. . . .

We get our first glimpse of the bride, a beautiful young woman, dressed in a white strapless wedding gown whose train gets dragged through the dirt. I never do get to meet the groom, although I am told he works in New York City for Africom.

Around 10:30, the entire party proceeds to city hall on foot, by *moto*, car, truck or van. The bridal couple is driven in a large, shiny limousine decorated with ribbons (Who in the hell owns this monstrosity?). Our little group of *tubabus* goes by van, and Guantanamo has to stop the traffic to lead me across the street on his arm. There must be 200 people, including several *griots* and young men pounding on tom toms.

City hall is just that: a huge hall, filled to standing room only. It is hot and airless. A young man gives me his seat. After the beribboned mayor enters the hall and clears out the well wishers who crowd around the table where the bride and groom are seated I notice that there are THREE bridal parties, not just one: Two of the bridal couples are in western attire (elaborate white wedding dresses for the women and dark suits for the men); one bride is totally in black, except for a tastefully draped pink scarf around her shoulders. Only her face is uncovered, compared with the naked shoulders and arms of her fellow brides. Her future husband is dressed in a dark suit as well.

Since the civil ceremony is totally in Bambara I can't understand much except the names and the "awo" (yes). The spectators laugh several times out loud, and I assume it is when the couples have to declare officially "before the law" whether their union is to be monogamous or polygamous. However, given my misinterpretation of the *griot* earlier this morning, they might have laughed at something else. Later I confirm that two of the couples opted for monogamy (until further notice) and one for polygamy. Using my cultural stereotypes, it is not difficult to figure out which couple did what.

We return to the compound and after a while and some soft drinks and water, the men (many fewer than females) and women separate. Men go to the adjoining street on the left, and women to the adjoining street to the right of the compound. Both streets are blocked off to motor traffic by huge dusty tents, specially erected for the occasion, filled with dusty chairs (for the women) and upholstered and lawn furniture (for the men). The women's side gets the music, a seven-piece percussion ensemble. One of the drummers is a cute boy, probably younger than my grandson, but already quite an accomplished drummer.

The loud-mouthed *griot* of the morning is now joined by several singing female *griots*. Their function seems to be to serve as masters of ceremony, entertainers, historians and praise singers. The call and response tradition of the *griots* reminds me of a service in a Southern U.S. Baptist church. Even MY ancestry gets praised. I have no idea of what is being said, but having observed what the Malians do whose heritage got acclaimed, I give the *griot* 1,000 CFA. Later I find out that the griot had praised my Cuban heritage since he thought I belonged to the Cuban contingent of our group. Oh, well, what you don't all have to do for world peace. . . .

There are women of all ages. Quite a number of the institute's students as well as local younger men have chosen the women's side of the festivities where the action (i.e., the dancing) is taking place.

The dusty circle around which the women sit several chairs deep gets sprinkled with water. The dancing begins, at first a fairly sedate circle dance of only women, which Guantanamo, the institute's driver, gets me to join. When the rhythm gets hotter the young ones (males and females) take over. At first I think the movements are spontaneous, but then it registers that there is a certain choreography and all dancers (young women as well as young men) perform the same movements: flailing arms, gyrating hips, high jumps! The rhythm is mesmerizing and the energy is absolutely amazing! Adrenalin takes over and they perform athletic feats. Soon the men's as well as the women's festive attire show their exertion by the tell-tell wetness in their armpits.

One of my male students simulates a dancing female, with a pink handbag under his arm. He really gets into the act with closed eyes and exaggerated, suggestive pelvic and hand movements. Some appreciative women hand him CFA notes. Given the (official) taboo against homosexuality in the Moslem world, I don't quite know whether this female impersonation should be taken positively or negatively. He seems to be pleased when I later tell him that he was dancing better than the women, but I still don't know whether his performance was a parody or a coming-out ceremony.

At 2 p.m. there is still no sign of food. Some of the Cubans go across the street to buy bananas and bread. My own cultural conditioning forbids me to bring my own food to a wedding feast, and I wait.

Finally, Bagayogo comes and leads the *tubabus* to the compound of his sister "where we can eat more comfortably." Several communal bowls are delivered filled with samé (rice with a delicious vegetable sauce and big chunks of boiled beef). Bagayogo gives us the choice of eating by hand or with a spoon. Not having washed my hands since morning, and having pressed dozens of hands I declare

Mali a free country and opt for a spoon. Though finally we all get a chance to wash our hands in a bucket of water, two of the Cubans opt for spoons as well and praise me for my courage. However, the only way to get the meat off the bones is by hand, and Bagayogo does so expertly, mushing the meat off the bones with his right hand only.

Around 4:30 p.m., Guantanamo drives us back to Bamako. Unfortunately, I did not get to observe what may be—for *tubabus*—the most interesting part of a Malian wedding: the rituals accompanying the religious ceremony at the mosque.

Am I losing it? Part II
Tuesday, February 13

TODAY WAS THE first time in my long teaching career that I lost control of a class! And it was not with pre-schoolers, with adolescents or with freshmen in college. It was with my advanced conversation course at CECJ—20 adult university students or working professionals who are paying the Center to improve their English.

I have structured the course so that each participant makes a short presentation on a self-selected topic, followed by discussion. Today, three students were scheduled to speak. One male student talked about "tourism highlights in Mali," and a female student talked about "increasing the leadership of women in the political process in Mali." We never got to student number three.

Talking about strident chauvinism! Yes, siree, "women's place is in the home, serving her man"—just as the Koran (and the Bible) have dictated! "Religion (Islam), culture and tradition confirm that Malian woman is not the equal of man." Since the man is in charge of decision making, "what would happen if his wife were active in politics and she did not share his opinion or did not do what he wanted her to do?"

The poor woman presenter tried her best to appease the three or four males who dominated the discussion. The three remaining women in class did not come to her aid—it is unclear whether because of lack of English proficiency, lack of an opinion or fear. Her most strident opponent was a fairly articulate English teacher at a *lycée*—a Dogon. No wonder! When I visited Dogon Country, I saw that they still banish women to menstruation huts during their period.

The student who was advocating for increased female political participation (she had studied accounting) was far from what Gloria Steinem would call "a liberated woman." She agreed that, indeed, "women are not equal to man," but that they are only complementary. And she fully agreed that "the man needs to be the decision maker and provider for the family." A heated discussion ensued.

Since I see myself mostly as facilitator of the discussion and don't want to dominate it, I refrained from expressing an opinion—even though it almost killed me. . . . But in spite of getting up and raising my voice, I could not regain control of the class to resume a semi-democratic process of discussion give-and-take. The class became total chaos, all hollering at once, and I was afraid it would come to physical blows.

I packed up my belongings. I shouted that what they practiced here was not democracy, but anarchy! That in the year 2012, equal rights and opportunity before the law, in education, in the work force, and in the political process was not a question of religion, culture or tradition but of basic human rights. And I left the class thirty minutes early.

They were dumb struck. Several of the students ran after me (one of them was another Dogon—which just tells you that not all of them are asses) apologizing profusely for their behavior. I felt like resigning my position, but it was 7:30 p.m. and Sister Rosalie (the director of CECJ) had already gone. So I took a taxi home, had a drink and went to bed.

This is one of those times when I feel hopeless about Mali's development which is clearly dependent on changing the role and rights of and opportunities for women. But maybe, what I experienced tonight was not so different from what American women experienced about 90 years ago when suffragists fought to get the vote in the U.S. Malian women do have the right to vote, but it may take several generations before their human rights in other areas get protected. *Insha Allah!*

Life as a roadie

February 16 to 18

This week is the Festival sur le Niger in Segou, a huge international music festival with already an established eight-year tradition. Hillary, former Peace Corps Volunteer in Mali (20 years ago), PH.D. in ethnomusicology from the University of Indiana, and currently on a Fulbright scholarship to teach and do research at the art institute will be one of the performers, and the only American featured on the program. When I told her that it was impossible to find accommodations in Segou (I tried already in November!), she offers me to come with her all-Malian band and serve as her assistant.

* * *

Already the night before our departure for Segou Hillary is all stressed out, because the balafon (similar to a xylophone) player sent her an SMS, demanding twice the money than he originally agreed to. Furthermore, he wants 50,000 CFA (about $100) to drive his old Mercedes the 230 km to Segou, although van transportation from Bamako to Segou has been arranged by the festival organizers for all the musicians. This happens after umpteen rehearsals and two nights before the performance! Hillary lets him hang without response and starts exploring the use of an alternate musician—a traditional flutist.

Although Hillary had hoped for "private" transportation for just her group, we have to get ourselves by taxi to the Tour d'Afrique where we are crammed together with other groups and their instruments into a mini-bus. We sit in the hot, airless bus, but the announced 1 p.m. departure still has not taken place at 2 p.m. Hillary tries her most assertive self in French and Bambara to get the van to leave or to find out why we are not leaving, but in usual Malian tradition, you don't find out what is happening until it happens.

* * *

Shortly before dark we arrive at our lodgings, the dormitories of a technical school for textile production about 5 km outside Segou. Our group of nine people (Hillary, her three back-up singers/dancers, the key board player, the balafon player, the djembe player, the drummer and I), is allotted four rooms, each with a double bed. Hillary tries to insist on the terms of her contract which specified single rooms for all the musicians, but nothing can be done.

Hillary makes arrangements to stay with the festival organizer who is a personal friend, so I get to occupy our dilapidated room and matrimonial bed by myself. The linoleum floor seems to have been cleaned last when Ramses II was building his pyramid. And let's not even talk about the two stand-up toilets and one shower shared by two dozen people!

Shortly after Hillary's departure to her new quarters, she calls me, totally distraught. She has left her camera bag with a new $1,000 Canon on the van that brought us to Segou. The van and driver have, of course, left long ago, and none of us knows the driver's name. I promise to do what I can.

A refurbished *sotrama* takes the musicians and me to the festival grounds where we are each given a plate of couscous with sauce and a spoon. After eating, Hillary's second in command, Vieux, and I go to the sound booth of the main stage and he calls everyone under the sun who may know the driver's name and have his phone number. If the camera is not found tonight (provided it is not already stolen), we can forget it.

The unbelievable happens! The driver found the camera bag and left it at some festival office. Vieux tells me to wait at the sound booth and promises to return after he hunts down the bag.

The musical performance scheduled for this evening starts only an hour late. The setting is quite impressive. The huge, open-air stage is actually set in the River Niger, and thousands of people face it, amphitheater-style, sitting on the ground or on the ubiquitous rental steel chairs. It seems all the whites in Mali are at the festival. I did not even realize there were that many.

Vieux (Hillary's second in command) never does come back to get me, but I have a good seat right behind the sound booth, offered to me by a young member of another Malian musical group. "We musicians" stick together, particularly since we are recognizable by the large badges we wear around our necks naming the group of which we are members, as well as the green plastic arm band which declares me "artiste 2012."

Moi, je suis l'assistante de Hillary, la chanteuse américaine. Most people, however, take me to be Hillary's mother, which I well could be, since she is my daughter's age. At first we try to explain our true relationship, but then it becomes too cumbersome and I remain "la maman de Hillary."

Around 11 p.m. I receive a message from Hillary that she has got the camera. Around 12:30 a.m. I try to round up whoever I can find and take the group by taxi back to our "luxury" lodgings.

Friday, February 17

Since I am free on Friday until the group's 4 p.m. sound check, I decide to explore Segou. There is no transportation back to town, but I hit the road anyway, hoping my age and my color will encourage one of the passing motorists to pick me up. And it works! In fact, the same friendly guy picks me up a second time when I stumble along the road in Segou, not having realized that the town—though it has fewer than 110,000 inhabitants—stretches along the Niger from hell to breakfast.

I decide to stop at the Motel Savane, which serves as some kind of conference headquarters, to try to get different accommodations for the remainder of the festival. No luck! But I run into several Peace Corps volunteers of my group who are camping in "bug huts" on the lawn in the courtyard of the motel. They offer to let me share their piece of ground covered by mosquito netting if I don't find anything else.

My young colleagues teach me how to save money by using the local motor cycle taxis which cost 100 CFA (about $-.20) and take you wherever you desire to go. I leave my colleagues who are off to use a hotel swimming pool near the festival grounds and explore the stalls of the "handitrash" sellers who surround the festival area.

Since Hillary wants us to meet for the sound check at

3:30 p.m., I take a motor cycle taxi back to my lodgings to pick up her instruments (a korah and three calabash drums) and return to the festival grounds with one of her musicians who came in his own car. Incidentally, the balafon player who requested a last-minute pay raise decided to come after all without such a raise. We are again served a meal (this time rice and sauce).

The sound check which was scheduled for 4 p.m. is more than 90 minutes late. I help by taking pictures (stage at sun set), and by wildly gesticulating to the band when the instrument or vocal sound is distorted. I am also supposed to find transportation for Hillary to get her back to her place for a change of clothes before the performance. Unfortunately, none of the numbers she has given me respond.

The sound check ends around 6:30, which leaves the band members only an hour and a half to return to their lodgings to change. Hillary tells us to return back stage by 7:45 p.m. Since I can stay in the grubby clothes that I have worn all day, I remain in town and rehydrate at a nearby Lebanese-owned restaurant.

* * *

I swear to Allah! If we *tubabus* are genetically predisposed to live within time frames, Malians lack that gene! The concept of punctuality and showing up at a predetermined time is simply meaningless for the majority of Malians.

8:00 p.m.: I am the first to arrive, though I, too, am late. 8 p.m. is listed on the program for the start of the performance. There are not yet very many spectators in front of the stage.

8:15 p.m.: Hillary arrives soon after me, obviously upset. Apparently, she had problems getting back to the festival, and some band members called to tell her that they are still at their lodgings and lack transportation back to town. Others are at a restaurant eating or doing something else.

8:30 p.m.: The stage manager stops by the little, curtained-off "room" on the barge that serves as stage that has been given our group "back stage," and asks when we are ready to start. Hillary tells him she has no musicians and complains about the lack of regular transportation from the dormitories to the festival site.

9:00 p.m. The stage manager stops by again to ask whether we are ready. Hillary is visibly upsets. Given the shoddy arrangements, she now wonders whether she will be paid after the concert so that she can, in turn, pay her musicians. She is on the phone non-stop. I feel totally helpless and am concerned about whether Hillary will be able to perform in her present mental state.

9:10 p.m.: Four of the six musicians finally arrive. One is still at the dormitory, since the driver could only take along four persons. And no one knows where the djembe player is. Rumors are rife that he is having dinner at the Motel Savane. Hillary is getting testy with her crew, and I can't keep my mouth shut either, lecturing the band members present that time is not a renewable resource, that their lateness wastes the time of others and is a sign of disrespect for those who are punctual. They use all kinds of excuses and simply don't understand that their reputation with the festival organizer, as well as future work opportunities (at least those with Hillary) are at stake.

9:30 p.m.: Charles, the young male singer/dancer who was left behind at the dormitory arrives.

9:45 p.m.: Hillary decides on starting the performance without the djembe player, although this African type of drum is considered essential for her musical selections. I am told to wait for the djembe player and tell him "to get his ass on stage ASAP after he arrives."

9:50 p.m.: The band starts playing to a full "house." Hillary's show is quite unique, since she has expertly fused American jazz selections with traditional Bambara music. She plays the korah and sings in English as well as Bambara which she still speaks quite fluently, although her Peace Corps service in Mali ended more than 20 years ago. There are some minor glitches, but Hillary and her band are enthusiastically received, and the audience never notices that the star of the show was ready to kill her musicians just some minutes ago. . . . They don't even notice the djembe player, who sneaks on stage late and did not have time to dress in the "uniform" that Hillary had bought for her band members. I am a wreck! I must have all those "time genes" that Malians are lacking. . . .

10:45 p.m.: I had planned to treat the group to a cele-bratory drink after a successful performance, but decide to just invite Hillary who is full of adrenalin and wound-up like an alarm clock. She reminds me quite a bit of myself when I was her age, including her complicated love life. . . .

February 18, 2012

Given the dreadful accommodations and experience of the day before, I decide to return to Bamako already on Saturday rather than on Sunday. Furthermore, my stomach tells me that I probably should not have eaten the delicious home-made frozen yoghurt that was recommended by one of my young Peace Corps colleagues, and was sold by a woman vendor out of her front door.

Anyway, together with two of Hillary's musicians who are both students at the institute I opt to return to Bamako by van provided by the festival organizers. I am the only *tubabu* and one of only four women in the crowded vehicle. And wonders never cease: We leave only half an hour after the scheduled 9 a.m. departure.

The air that comes through the small slits in the windows for ventilation feels like coming from a furnace. The landscape passing the windows clearly shows that it hasn't seen a drop of rain since last October. Everything is brown and covered by layers of dust, and many of the few trees and bushes along the road have lost their foliage. And it will be about four months before the start of the next rainy season! The dust collects in small hard bullets in my nostrils.

My throat is dry. I am awfully thirsty but am afraid to drink the water I am carrying, because I don't want to have to pee. (Finding a *njegen* on the way to Segou was a semi-catastrophe.) I have great admiration for the toughness of the people who exist in this climate and landscape, but wonder for the umpteenth time, why they did not continue their trek and settle in more hospitable surroundings. But then, why did the Tohono O'Odhams or the Yaquis not leave the Sonoran semi-desert of the Arizona/Mexico borderlands and move on to Illinois?

When I finally arrive at my apartment, 230 km and five hours later, I am totally dehydrated and consume about a gallon of water, koolaid, beer, tonic water and everything else liquid I can find in my little refrigerator. I am glad to be home.

An ode to Bamako taxi drivers

My MAIN MEANS of transportation in Bamako is by taxi. So far, since arriving in the capital city of Mali last August, I have experienced two flat tires; we ran out of gasoline once, and I needed to wait in the taxi until the chauffeur came back with a bottle of gas to help get us to a gas station; two drivers had to hot-wire the ignition to get their jalopy going; once we had to be pushed to jump start the engine; and already three times I witnessed with my own eyes my taxi driver bribing a police officer who had stopped us—once to check our papers and once because the taxi had a missing head light; I don't know what was wrong the third time. I estimate that less than 25% of the taxis have windshields that are not cracked. And on maybe half of the vehicles the door opening latch or window opening mechanism no longer work. The absolute highlight, however, was when I entered the taxi, slammed the door shut, and the door fell off. . . .

Twice the police tried to flag down my taxi to stop for a document check, but the driver instead stepped on the gas. The first time I expected to hear a pursuing siren within two minutes and I ducked to avoid any possible bullets from pursuing cops. . . . But nothing happened.

At least one of the taxi drivers was totally illiterate, and I wondered how he got a license (or whether he even had one). And one driver gave sufficient evidence by his erratic driving and belligerent attitudes toward other drivers (and even to the traffic police) that he was clearly under the influence of something. But so far, I arrived in one piece at all my planned destinations—eventually!

Taxis here have no meters, and you better agree on a fare before departure! The first fare quoted is usually a *tubab* fare, at least 1,000 CFA (about $2.00) above what a Malian would pay. Sometimes, when I am not already exhausted from the heat and dust, I make a big fuss, insisting that I work here and want to be treated like a *Mali muso* (Malian woman) and not a *tubabu* and that usually does the trick.

I usually sit in front with the driver to permit him to pick up other fares. Most "taximans" are quite friendly and delighted when I use my few words of Bambara. When one asks me for my Malian name (Salimata Diarra), I can just hope that the driver is not named Traoré, or he will start a big fuss, insisting that I need to change my name to Traoré, because the Diarras are "amayn" (bad), while the Traorés are "akayn" (good). They accuse me of being a "bean eater" (which, is considered an insult here) and one Traore stopped on the side of the road and threat-

ened to throw me out of his taxi (in jest, of course), and another one offered marriage to change my name (in jest, of course). All this jesting is part of the tradition of "joking cousins," (*sanankouja*) quite unique to Mali and seriously practiced by most people. If your name is Coulibaly, you are lucky, because everyone gets along with you, but, unfortunately, the Diarras are not so popular, even though they come from the royal "caste."

Open Sesame! Episode #2
Thursday, February 23

THE MISERABLE LOCK on my front door that had already been replaced once last November has again given up the ghost. Thanks to Allah, this time it happened with me inside the apartment and the door open. I called Bagayogo, but, of course, nothing can be done on short notice. I can still lock the flimsy screen door, but otherwise I and my belongings can be easily accessed by anyone who has a mind to. I make a great show of pretending to lock both doors when leaving and entering the apartment while the neighboring maids are washing clothes outside on the walk way, so no one catches on that my place is open. At night I place a chair in front of the door. This way I should at least hear it if someone tries to enter.

Friday, February 24

I go to work, still with a broken lock. But I do take

along my lap top and camera, pretty much the only things I would really miss if they were stolen. Bagayogo promises to send someone to fix the lock this afternoon.

* * *

Today is my birthday. I did not tell anyone, but—just by chance—Lili and Louisa, my two former Cuban neighbors from my Guarantigibougou—Nerekoro days have invited Hillary and me for lunch at their place. They, too, have moved closer to town and now live in a dilapidated apartment building worse than my own.

Lili, Louisa, two of their male Cuban friends, Hillary and I have a delicious lunch (*arroz con frijoles*, pork chops and salad) and when I fess up to this day being my birthday, the lunch turns into an impromptu birthday party with Spanish and English versions of the "happy birthday" song.

I so much wish that we could communicate better. The Cubans speak little English and barely enough French to survive. And, unfortunately, ever since I arrived in Mali and am forced to communicate in either French or Bambara, my Spanish conversational ability has pretty much abandoned me. I still understand much, but the Cubans speak like machine guns, and swallow their final "s's," so I usually cannot get beyond comprehending the barest of context when they talk to each other. Trying to speak Spanish at present is slow and painful and I generally avoid it. This phenomenon of "language loss" of the language you are least competent in when you try to learn a new one is quite common. The Cubans tell me they have the same experience, having lost whatever English competence they had while trying to learn French.

* * *

Late afternoon the lock repair man finally arrives—the same guy who came last November, and he installs the same rinkydink piece of Chinese junk (I can bend the key with my fingers) that gave up the ghost after barely three months of use. I suggested that he get a better quality lock, but am told they are too expensive.

Open Sesame! Episode #3

February 27

ONE OF MY courses at the institute was again cancelled without notification. I don't know why. Will I ever get used to finding out what is happening only after it has happened?

I am lucky to catch a ride back to town so I don't have to wait 2 ½ hours for the van to take me back to the apartment. But when I try to open the front door, the newly installed lock does not budge. I push, pull, shove, pound, rattle, but the key is stuck and does not move. I call Bagayogo and tell him in as polite French as I am capable of that if you install shitty parts you get shitty results. I am too mad to understand his full response, but he promises to send someone to help me get into my place.

I wait outside my apartment on the third floor walk way under the merciless sun of the Sahel. I wait. It is now shortly after noon and very hot. I wait, and wait some more. I try again to push, kick, rattle and pull on the door, and—lo and behold—the key turns and the door opens. I do not inform Bagayogo of this lucky development since the lock still needs repair. But by 5 p.m. still no one from the institute has shown up and for all they know, I might still be waiting in front of my door.

Now, all the neighbors in my block know, of course, that I can't lock my door. I contact the Peace Corps with my tale of woe. They can't do anything tonight but will send someone first thing in the morning. Again, I barricade myself with a chair against the door before retiring under my mosquito net. But I am not overly worried. I am sure that if I scream, the entire neighborhood will converge and beat the hell out of anyone I accuse of wrong doings. I heard that a pick-pocket in the local market was almost beaten to death. This ain't the U.S., where bystanders are reluctant to interfere, or New York City where no one appears to give a damn when you are attacked.

February 28

The American tax payer will be happy to know that my front door now has a Vachette lock, "the global leader in door opening solutions," installed with the help of three Peace Corps staff.

Living high on the hog

March 6

Ahhhhh, the good life! I am cat-sitting for the U.S. Ambassador for two weeks while she is in the States. I assume that I got recommended for the job because I may not be as prone as my younger colleagues are to use this opportunity for hosting wild parties and emptying the well equipped bar and wine collection.

There is air conditioning! Windows with window glass! Hot water coming out of faucets! A pool! The living room is the size of Grand Central Station with a baby grand piano. The formal dining room seats at least a small battallion. The hotel-sized modern kitchen is equipped with stoves and refrigerators to feed hundreds (clean, clean, clean!). There are several bathrooms with toilet seats. There are several (functioning) TVs. Apart from the Ambassador, the occupants are four household staff (not counting security), and two cats. All this is surrounded by a well maintained green lawn and high walls.

I can read at night without wearing a head lamp! And I am sleeping without mosquito net on a real mattress rather than on a lumpy piece of foam! I am in charge of a huge key collection (every door is keyed differently) and am somewhat paranoid at night after the household staff leaves and when it's only me and the cats in this huge, stately residence that is used to entertaining politicians (U.S. as well as Malian), industrialists, bankers and others who want to make a buck in Mali, military personnel to help the Malian army fight Al Qaeda, representatives of the American cultural scene, NGOs who hope to spend some U.S. tax money on do-good causes or people who for some other reason need to be impressed by American hospitality.

I am not envious of the Ambassador's life. Life is

easier in the Peace Corps where you are much less encumbered by formal traditions and "stuff," and can put your feet on the living room furniture, provided you have any, and there are no Malians present who consider the view of someone's soles a taboo.

There is music on the note stand next to the grand piano, though no one plays the piano. The coffee-table books cover a wide range of topics from *Historic Homes in New England* (I wonder if anybody gives a damn about these in Mali?) to *American Silver* to *Artisanat de tradition en Amérique*, all carefully chosen to present the best America has to offer. For whatever reason, there is also a huge coffee table volume entitled *Sur la terre de dinosaures.*

I am pleased that the Ambassador has decorated the place with many personal photographs, or else I would feel like I lived in the middle of *Homes and Gardens* or another home decorating magazine.

Supposedly the electronic security does not work, but something peeps at me whenever I pass in certain places. I would not be surprised if I were under surveillance, even though I am quite sure my level of patriotism was checked before I was asked to do the job. . . .

The large place feels a little creepy after the departure of "my" household staff, although I am probably safer here than I have ever been in my life. All of the many doors and windows are protected by heavy rod iron security screens with double locks (including a bolt lock on each door). I am checking them all every night (eleven doors alone in the downstairs living area).

At all times, there are at least three Malian guards (two armed and in military fatigues, and one in civilian duds) in front of the heavy steel door that protects the compound, and another two in front of the gate leading to the car park. I am surprised there is no U.S. Marine, but the Ambassador explained that they only protect classified material at the Embassy.

In spite of the heavy protection I lock up the "official downstairs" and retire to the Ambassador's upstairs personal quarters with Mickey and Minnie, my feline companions.

It takes me awhile to find something else than AFN and the Pentagon Channel on TV, but finally I discover CNN, though the connection is poor. After half an hour of watching what is supposedly new in the world I decide that I haven't missed that much in the last nine months that I have been in Mali. And I am ever so glad that I don't have to experience the absolute ridiculous U.S. pre-election hysteria on a day-to-day basis! When I get back to America, I will lobby Congress to limit pre-election politicking to three months before the election, like they do in civilized places, such as Mali!

March 9

I can't wait until Saturday and Sunday, when "my" household staff is off and I have the place to myself. I can't get used to their silently padding around the house and "sneaking up" on me lying on the couch, giving me barely enough time to pull my skirt down. But I know already that I will dearly miss the air conditioning as well as the mattress when I will need to move back to my own digs. And I will miss the quiet.

Although, comparing my new place of residence to my Peace Corps digs, it appears that I have died and gone to heaven, I realize that there is little here that one would not find in a middle class American household (except the industrial-sized kitchen and huge collection of dishes and silverware!). In fact, my Tucson residence offers more comfort and practicality than this Grand Central Station.

* * *

I have invited Hillary to come for lunch and swimming tomorrow.

Two major victories

March 13

FOR THE SECOND day in a row the media center at the institute is occupied and my classes are moved half an hour late to the main classroom building. The electricity is working again in my former classroom and I can see my students' faces, but both yesterday and today I had to send students out to search for chairs and a board to write on. Why does this lack of organization and communication still frustrate me after six months?

One of my Spanish colleagues just sits outside and waits for "better weather" when his classroom is occupied or his students don't show up. He tells me he is doing his job just by being here. If they don't take advantage of it, it is their problem. Unfortunately, even if I would not have to feel guilty because my living allowance here is paid with U.S. taxpayers' hard earned money, my personality traits do not permit me to take this same course of action. So, again, I feel helpless and am seething with frustration. Things improve, however, later that day with two major victories:

Victory #1: I received an e-mail from the U.S. Embassy that both of the students I had nominated for a six-week program in the U.S. this coming summer have been awarded the coveted scholarship. I am delighted!

Victory #2: One of the topics featured in today's evening advanced conversation course at the CECJ is excision, aka female circumcision or female genital mutilation (FGM). The young woman who presents the topic reads from some script (as usual, without citing the source), and is barely understandable. After she finishes there are very few questions or comments. Those who comment appear to accept that religion and tradition justify this mutilation. I don't know whether her fellow students also had problems understanding what she was saying, whether the topic is taboo or of no interest.

I am just about ready to move to the next student and topic ("Road accidents in Mali") when one of the two physicians in the class gets up and asks for permission to make some explanations. He goes to the board, draws the outline of a vagina, graphically illustrates what happens during excision, and in halting English explains why the procedure can be a hazard to women's health. He has everyone's undivided attention, but it is obvious that not all students can follow his explanation.

One of the males asks whether it would be possible that the physician repeat his explanations in French, since he would like to fully understand. Some students object to the need for switching to French, but I am absolutely elated that a Malian (and yet a male! And yet a physician!) supports what I have been trying surreptitiously to say all along. I declare "time out for French for two minutes."

The young physician factually describes the frequent by-products of female circumcision: terrible pain (since the procedure is done without anesthesia); major loss of blood; shock (at times leading to death); infection (caused by unsanitary "surgical" conditions and ignorance of traditional practitioners); incontinence; difficulties in giving birth because of weakened scar tissue where the clitoris was removed, or in cases where the vagina has grown shut and needs to be surgically reopened; frigidity; etc. Interestingly, he does not plead—as I generally do—for a total end to this barbaric, painful, traumatizing, and medically totally unnecessary procedure. Instead, he advocates to replace the current practices of FGM with just a "ritual cutting" which gives its due to tradition but leaves the female genital apparatus in tact.

I recognize the strength of local traditions and the wisdom of his words and keep my mouth shut. In my rational moments, I realize that cultural change occurs very slowly, particularly if the changes advocated are not encouraged or supported by legislation and frequent sound bytes in the media.

Many of the students have become thoughtful, and even my two Dogons, who always have the last word, do not object to what has been said. I have the feeling that tonight may have been my most useful contribution to Malian development. . . .

March 19

I am still living "high on the hog" at the Ambassador's. I have established a routine, and life is almost boring. I have even given a dinner party, utilizing, of course, the services of the cook! But I am getting ready for the local equivalent of "spring break" with a trip to Ghana to meet my friend Al who will be coming from Tucson. Since he is an old Ghana hand, having worked as a mining geologist in that country on numerous occasions, I am looking forward to having an experienced guide to this former British colony (English is the "official" language) and predominantly Christian nation. We will be in Ghana from March 21 to April 1.

Part IV *The end*

(written after evacuation from
Mali and return to Tucson)

All through the French interregnum, the Tuareg
resisted, essentially ungoverned and ungovern-
able, but the ancient trading towns of Mali and
Songhai, Djenné and Timbuktu and Gao continued their awful decay—their raisons d'être
vanished, their trade gone, their academies closed,
their populations static or shrinking. To the
imperial power in faraway Paris, Mali ... [was]
of such fundamental unimportance that nearly
half of all civil service positions were empty at any
given time. Indeed, French officials were often
assigned there as punishment.

—Marq de Villiers and Sheila Hirtle,
Timbuktu—The Sahara's Fabled City of Gold

My daughter tells me that I can't just stop cold with my Mali journal entries. She has shared my adventures with too many of her friends who now wonder what has happened to me. So, here is the last chapter.

Off to spring break in Ghana
Wednesday, March 21

HILLARY'S *TAXIMAN*, OUSMAN, picked me up at the U.S. Ambassador's residence punctually at 6 a.m. for the trip to the Bamako airport. Ethiopian Airlines, flight 908 left on time at 8:50 a.m. for Lomé, Togo, where I needed to change to Asky flight 10 to Accra, Ghana. At the time I did not realize that my last experiences in Mali actually happened on time, as scheduled. This should already have served as a bad omen!

* * *

The air conditioning was out at the Lomé airport. The huge departure hall was airless; the waiting passengers were visibly uncomfortable in spite of furiously fanning themselves with any article at hand. Why do tropical airports have to be hermetically sealed like those in colder places? Why can't they take advantage of the climate and leave the waiting rooms open to the air currents under shade-giving roofs? The answers to my frustrated questions are probably that the computers would not work in the local humidity, and the kerosene exhaust from the airplane engines would probably shorten the passengers' life span. But apart from the sweltering heat and a delay in the scheduled departure time the trip was uneventful.

* * *

If everything went as planned, Al was to pick me up at Kotoka Airport. But just in case, we had made arrangements to meet at the Shangrila Hotel near the airport, if his or my flight got delayed. But though the plane arrived almost 90 minutes late, there was Al, patiently standing outside customs, waiting for me. He did not have a choice: The hotel had recently changed names from Shangrila to Western Sun, and since he could not reach me to inform me of that fact, he was worried that we would not connect.

My first impressions of Accra and Southern Ghana, compared with Bamako and Mali, was that this place is "Africa Lite": Most people are dressed western style; tall, modern buildings; fancy hotels and restaurants; paved roads that are better maintained than those in Tucson, Arizona; huge bill boards advertising all kinds of worldly goods as well as Christian revival meetings, offered by every possible Christian sect from Apostolic to Zion. The bill boards feature black as well as white preachers who schedule themselves in football stadiums and other large venues to redeem the sinful masses. Those gatherings must be lucrative!

There are construction sites after construction sites. And, praise be to Allah! there are very few motorcycles and much fewer of the dilapidated vehicles (imported from the European used car market) than one encounters in Mali. Even the traffic flows relatively smoothly. I experienced no U-turns in the middle of the block.

But just to ruin the illusion of being north of the 30th degree of latitude, we had to change hotel rooms three times in 24 hours because of malfunctioning appliances or non-functioning utilities.

Friday, March 23

Al does not believe like I do, that it builds character and is an enriching experience when travelling Peace Corps style (i.e., on local public transport crammed in with chickens and goats), so he had made arrangements with his former driver, Paul Tetteh, to take us on a tour along the coast (Elmina, Kakum National Park, Cape Coast, Ankobra Beach, Nzulezo village on stilts) and in-land (via Kumasi to Mole National Park, back to Kumasi and Akwatia Diamond Mine) in the north western and central parts of the country. Paul picked us up punctually at the hotel in his freshly polished Honda. I could only marvel "what a difference a day makes" when travelling from Mali to Ghana.

The coup

UNFORTUNATELY, THE REST of the trip to Ghana has pretty much become a blur, because that evening I found out that shortly after my departure from Bamako (in fact, around noon that same day), there was a military coup in Mali. President Amadou Toumani Touré (ATT) was nowhere to be found, a number of ministers were being detained at Kati—the Malian equivalent of Westpoint—, the Malian constitution had been suspended, ORTM (Mali TV) had been taken over by the soldiers, the airport and borders had been closed, stores and banks were shuttered, a 24-hour curfew had been declared.

My first reaction was disbelief. Peace Corps volunteers had been told repeatedly that Mali served as a model for emergent democracies in Africa. Presidential elections were scheduled for April 29 and lo and behold, ATT had for some time declared that he would step down after his second term in office (as specified by the constitution), contrary to other African political leaders who determine to become "president for life" and who want to establish dynasties (e.g., Libya, Tunisia, Egypt, Ivory Coast, Senegal, Zimbabwe, Congo, etc., etc.) after they have tasted power and wealth.

What was happening to my Peace Corps colleagues? What was happening to my students? What was happening to my neighbors?

Saturday, March 24

I was getting awfully frustrated by the lack of coverage by the American media of the political upheaval in Mali. Damn it! Why are we so preoccupied with local trivia and so little concerned by what is happening in the rest of the world? This upheaval was a catastrophe for over 13 Million people—not counting myself and about 200 American volunteers!—and I couldn't find coverage on CNN!!!! Thanks to Allah for Al Jazeera that provided daily updates of what was happening in Mali. (Parenthetically, even after returning to Tucson and searching the newspaper for news about Mali, I find coverage of "Calif. 'rudest waiter' eatery may stay open after all," and of "Dairymen Protest in India" (*Arizona Daily Star*, 4/22/2012), but nothing about the tragedy happening south of the Sahara. There was some coverage of Syria and the Sudan, but Mali, so far, had not attracted the attention of any American movie stars....

I watched an interview—conducted in English—with the leader of the putsch, a Captain Amadou Sanogo, and was shocked to note that the s.o.b. speaks good English! I hoped he did not learn it in the U.S. (he did!). He stated as reason for the rebellion the war in the North and ATT's lack of support for the military to stand up to the Tuareg fighters. But, unfortunately, even without ATT, the Malian military could not defeat the Tuareg rebels either. Al Jazeera reported that Timbuktu, Kidal and Gao had fallen to them. There were reports of rapes, murders, looting and grizzly mutilations up north, and violence and looting in Bamako. I hoped that the new lock on the door to my apartment detered any efforts to get to "my stuff."

Sunday, March 25

Although I could no longer make calls on my Malian cell phone in Ghana, I still could receive SMSs from Peace Corps. We were told to go into consolidation (i.e., essentially a lock down of volunteers in regional capitals). We were also asked to call our families, since concerned parents apparently were swamping the phone lines at Peace Corps Washington wondering about their offspring. I found a computer and sent an e-mail to Peace Corps Mali for instructions on when to come back. I was directed to stay in Ghana until further notice.

Thursday, March 29

The SMSs from Peace Corps Mali were alternately optimistic and pessimistic. Some Volunteers in the western part of the country were permitted to return to their sites. Volunteers in Bamako still needed to sit tight except for going to buy food at the nearest *alimentation*. But volunteers in the Mopti region (near Timbuktu) were evacuated. (One of my young Mopti colleagues later told me during the transition conference in Ghana that he hid in a beauty parlor to avoid the shooting in the streets, and that his regional director came on his motorcycle to rescue him eventually. I kidded him that now I knew why he had to go home: It was because he flaunted Peace Corps rules against riding on a motorcycle....)

More and more foreign embassies were closing in Mali and sending home all "non essential personnel." Various American and European NGOs were dismantling their operations and leaving the country. This war and the military coup were setting Mali back at least twenty years in development. Let's not even mention the humanitarian tragedy in Northern Mali with over 200,000 refugees!

I was touched by how many people were starting to worry about me. My Nigerian goddaughter recommended that I return to the U.S. immediately, "because Africans can be very crude in situations like this." My daughter tells me that some of her friends were becoming experts on Mali and scouring the internet for news. And my granddaughter may be the only 7th grader who knew the name of the capital city of Mali.

***

I was beginning to get directions directly from Peace Corps Washington. Apparently Peace Corps Mali had enough to do without dealing with volunteers outside the country. Did I need anything? Did I have enough money to pay for hotel accommodations? I was to get in touch with Peace Corps Ghana Security and keep them informed of my whereabouts.

I could not but admire the finely honed bureaucracy and communication system of the Peace Corps. It is geared to work in *loco parentis* for a bunch of nubile and hormone ridden college grads. I told Washington that I had a tooth brush and a credit card and not to worry. But it felt good to have an entire government agency in DC concerned about little old me....

In my lucid moments I was angry at myself for worrying about "my stuff" in Bamako while there was a humanitarian crisis in progress. But I nevertheless emailed Peace Corps Mali and inquired whether someone could at least try to get my laptop from my apartment. If they didn't, this meant that I would have lost two laptops in Mali within a period of six months. And my first loss still had not taught me to regularly back up all my data on an external hard drive.... Peace Corps Mali responded that they would try.

I was pretty sure that the laptop was safe. Before my

departure, I had hidden it behind my dilapidated living room couch so it would be hard to find, even if the apartment was broken into.

Friday, March 30

Al and I returned to Accra. I received an email messages from Hillary, as well as from several American non-Peace Corps acquaintances that they had decided to leave Mali. Allah have mercy! Was the situation getting that bad?

Stranded in Accra

Saturday, March 31

I HAD ORIGINALLY booked my return to Bamako on April 1, but Peace Corps Washington directed me to rebook my return flight for the following week. No one had local phone numbers for the airlines. So, the Acting Director of Peace Corps Ghana sacrificed her Saturday afternoon and took me to the airport for the rebooking. The Asky Airline office was in chaos and rebooking the flight took four hours! Despite the trappings of "modernity," we were still in Africa! I reminded myself to remain patient. "Modern," technologically-driven life in Europe and North America had developed organically. That is, the change from an agrarian society to an industrialized one proceeded relatively slowly, and the people had time to get used to planes, phones, computers, ATMs, etc. It was not impossible that the people trying to help me at the airport never had been on a plane, or that they had not even seen a computer when they left their native villages for an education and work in Accra.

Sunday, April 1

Al was flying back to Tucson today. Peace Corps Ghana picked us up from the hotel and took us to what was to be my residence while waiting for news from Mali: the large walled compound and empty two-story house of a former Peace Corps Medical Officer who had returned to the U.S. The place was in the process of renovation and was unfurnished except for a bed, chest of drawers, and a micro wave, but the toilet flushed and the shower worked. I even found some sheets and two towels which had probably been used by the former occupants.

The house was located in an upscale residential neighborhood. From the street one could only see the high walls surrounding the neighboring compounds and the guards protecting them.

Monday, April 2

Hallelujah! In a message dispatched at 8:34 a.m I was informed that most Malian volunteers were being "deconsolidated" (i.e., those who had cell phone service at their sites could return to their "homes"), but they were to report in by SMS daily. The situation in Bamako was still "fluid," but I was told that I could return to Bamako on April 8. I was elated. Apparently the airport as well as land borders had been reopened.

Tuesday, April 3

With an SMS sent at 5:06 a.m. I was informed that Malian volunteers were "reconsolidated" (i.e., those who had left regional transit houses had to return and go back into lock down); volunteers in the Mopti region were evacuated. We were reminded to come with our "go-bags," including important papers, medications, water purifying tablets, phone cards, money and passports. Unfortunately, most of my important papers (e.g. driver's license, check books, some credit cards, tax records, etc.), as well as refills of my medications and my "civilian" passport were in Bamako.

* * *

The place I had been living in these past two days was just too far away from food and transportation. And even though there was a night guard watching over the premises, the big empty house and compound were somewhat eerie. So I decided to move to the Transit House at Peace Corps Accra headquarters.

Ghana had been the first Peace Corps program established world-wide in 1961, but compared with the transit house in Bamako, this was the slums! No TV! You can't even fry an egg! There was no wireless! But the place was close to "the action," and furthermore, I could ask my Ghanaian colleagues for advice on where to go and how to get there.

I moved into one of the three small rooms with four

stacked beds each. One young male gallantly moved his mess to the upper bunk bed so that I didn't have to climb the ladder to get to my sleeping space.

I was staying glued to El Jazeera whenever I got access to one of the three computers that were available for volunteer use. As the "refugee" from Peace Corps Mali, I was becoming somewhat of a celebrity.

* * *

By SMS sent at 12:06 p.m. I was informed that PC Mali was being evacuated. Most foreign embassies as well as foreign NGOs had already left; ECOWAS (Economic Community of West African States) had declared sanctions; borders were again closed; banking system were shut down. All that, as well as food and gasoline shortages and the accompanying price increases finally had convinced Peace Corps Washington that it was time to get the hell out of Dodge!

* * *

I am sure evacuation was not an easy decision. I could only guess at the amount of planning, time, effort, frustration, energy, work, personnel (not even mentioning MONEY) that it had taken to build up the current infrastructure to support almost 200 (mostly young) Americans strewn all over this vast nation who are valiantly trying to help Malians improve their health, environment, living conditions, and economic opportunities. I could only guess at what would happen to the approximately 60 Malians employed by Peace Corps who would suddenly have to join the vast ranks of the unemployed. I could only guess at what would happen to the buildings, equipment, vehicles, and support materials that had been acquired over the past 40 years that Peace Corps had served in Mali.

And what was happening to my Malian friends and students? Were they safe? Would my students lose an entire semester because I had left? Midterm exams had been scheduled for April 2 and 3. I was not even able to assign interim grades, because my records were in Bamako and I was in Ghana. I was supposed to give a public lecture at CECJ this week end, but assumed that the last thing on Malians' mind at present was attending lectures. I emailed the Education Program Coordinator in Bamako nevertheless that he should inform both the institute and CECJ that I would not be back in the near future. The e-mail was returned as being non-deliverable.

What would happen to Mariam and Fouseyni, the two students who had been awarded a scholarship to the U.S. this coming summer and for whom I had served as intermediary with the Embassy? What would happen with the summer language immersion program (English and French) for girls that I had been planning for next year?

I was on an emotional roller coaster and so upset that I was experiencing physical symptoms (heart palpitations, occasional shortness of breath and sleeping problems). Even my usual remedies against stress, such as walking around the block, talking to myself, going shopping or drinking Star beer did not help!

Evacuation

Thursday, April 5

THE TUAREG REBELS (MNLA) in the north proclaimed the territory they had won (the three northern regions of Kidal, Timbuktu and Gao as well as parts of Mopti) the independent state of Azawad and agreed to a cease-fire. Some infighting was reported among the various fundamentalist Islamic factions of the rebels, including Al Qaeda (AQIM) and Boko Haram. May Allah forgive me, but with some luck they will kill each other!

* * *

I was the first among my colleagues to find out that Peace Corps Mali was being evacuated via Accra. Peace Corps Ghana went into emergency mode, although it was Easter weekend with Good Friday and Easter Monday being public holidays in the south of this predominantly Christian country. (The north of Ghana is predominantly Moslem.) Ghana staff had 2 1/2 days to make arrangements to house and feed about 230 people, including volunteers, plus Malian and regional staff, as well as people arriving from headquarters in Washington. They needed to get a landing permit for the charter flight that would transport my colleagues from Bamako to Accra. They needed to expedite the visa process for the group. They needed to prepare for the five-day transition conference, including medical clearance, that would lead us to complete our Mali service (COS) and let us decide individually what we would do next with our disrupted lives.

I offered my help and got busy making copies and stuffing folders.

April 8

Arrival in Accra of 180 Mali Peace Corps volunteers with their worldly belongings, plus five staff, on a chartered Ethiopian Airlines plane. I was delighted to see that the remaining 18 volunteers of my group, named the Goodfellas (apparently because of our exemplary behavior during training), were alive and—at least physically—in good shape. I found out that I was not the only one who arrived in Ghana with a minimal supply of clothing and nothing else. Some had not been able to return to their sites after the first consolidation on March 25.

The Malian staff had brought along some of my belongings that I had prioritized in an e-mail message. Unfortunately, they did not bring priorities #1 and #2: my laptop and my income tax papers. They did, however, deliver a suitcase full of sheets, towels, fabric, and pot holders that I had acquired in Bamako (who the hell decided to bring that stuff???) and which I was able to distribute later to volunteers who decided to transfer to other sites.

April 9–13

It was obvious that Peace Corps staff have acquired prior experience in dealing with evacuations! I admired the efficiency and organization of how we were processed. We were shown understanding and empathy for our plight. We all had to complete the paper work to COS (completion of service). All of us had to have blood, urine and TB tests. All 180 of us had to meet individually with one of the medical staff to discuss present health conditions and get instructions of what medical follow up we needed to do after arriving in the States, since there was not enough time to de-worm and "debug" us (e.g., for Schistosomiasis and malaria). Those of us who so desired, could receive counseling from two psychologists flown in from Washington.

Given my age, my mechanisms for dealing with traumatic experiences are fairly well honed. But a number of my young colleagues clearly suffered from PTSD. You only had to look at them and they started crying. And if you hugged them they sobbingly clung to you for dear life.

The emotions displayed were not surprising, since many of the volunteers had become deeply integrated into their communities. Some had to leave behind pets. Some had found local boyfriends or girlfriends. And one had just been married to a Dogon the week before the coup.

Evacuated Mali volunteers had five choices: 1) They could ask for an immediate transfer to serve in another country; 2) they could ask for delayed transfer to another county which permitted them a short stay in the U.S. before continuing their service. 3) they could go home and wait for Mali Peace Corps to be reinstated; 4) they could go home and reapply for Peace Corps service elsewhere or apply for Peace Corps Response assignments; or 5) they could go home and forget about the Peace Corps.

I felt the need to regain control over my own life and didn't even consider an immediate transfer. I was somewhat tempted to apply for a delayed transfer, but my opportunities for transfer, given my area of specialty, were limited: Ethiopia (too close to Somalia!), Liberia (they suffered a Charles Taylor only about ten years ago!), and Mongolia (given the trauma of trying to learn Bambara at my age, trying to learn Mongolian would probably push me off the deep end! And furthermore, they have long, cold winters!). So I opted to COS and wait for possible reinstatement of PC Mali when I could complete the term of my service. I have learned so much, I have met so many great people, I left so many projects unfinished, I have seen such need, and I have felt so useful with the little I was able to accomplish. I would be happy to return.

Saturday, April 14, 2012

Return to Tucson—physically and emotionally exhausted.

Epilogue

ON JANUARY 28, 2013 an intervention by French military forces started to set Islamist fundamentalists in the north of Mali to flight. An estimated half a million people had been displaced by the civil war. On July 28, 2013, Mali held its first presidential and legislative elections after the coup. Twenty-eight candidates stood for election. A run-off election held on August 11, 2013 declared Ibrahim Boubakar Keïta the fifth Malian president since the country's independence.

Timbuktu and the northern regions are again open to trade and journalists. But reports of occasional kidnappings and suicide commandos indicate that security is still elusive. As of mid-2014, the U.S. Peace Corps has not returned to Mali. There are, however, explorations underway to re-open at least the agricultural, health and marketing sectors for Peace Corps Volunteers with prior experience in Mali.

As for the author, I have more or less re-adjusted to the complexities of American life. About six months after my return to the U.S. I did receive some of the personal belongings which I had to leave behind due to the emergency evacuation from Mali in April 2012. Let's hope that the many books and materials I left behind, as well as the clothes, kitchen inventory and acquired furniture found some appreciative users in the neighborhood.

After regaining my mental equilibrium I could not but reflect on whether my time in Mali had made any worthwhile contribution to the people of that country. Clearly, my successes at the art institute as English teacher—my main Peace Corps assignment—were practically nil. I never did develop effective mechanisms to deal with the general chaos and lack of interest on the part of many of the students. I am quite certain that I failed to be "the catalyst for change" that the Peace Corps wants its volunteers to be.

My success may have been greater teaching English and interacting with the participants of the conversation courses at the Centre d'Etude et de Culture pour Jeunes. Apart from any measurable gain in their English language fluency, I am convinced that our intensive discussions and explorations of sometimes controversial topics stimulated a number of course participants to evaluate their own beliefs and opinions and—if nothing else—developed some emerging understanding, and maybe acceptance of viewpoints other than those held previously.

The greatest impact I had probably through my informal participation in the English Language Club. I was delighted when in the spring of 2014 I received an email announcing that the Club was intending to revive the English language competition for local schools started in 2012 and asking me to review their materials for the event. It is with members of this group that I developed friendships and am continuing to be in frequent contact. They address me as "Dear Salimata" and assure me that "life in Bamako is normal." Mariam and Fouseyni informed me that they have started an organization called "Le movement pour le progrès de la femme."

Of course, all the plans for possible summer institutes for Malian girls or the workshops for teachers had to be abandoned when Peace Corps was evacuated.

The biggest beneficiary of my 11-months sojourn in Mali was undoubtedly I. I gained insights into a fascinating culture so different from my own. The experience strengthened my conviction that working jointly across cultures—often one-on-one—was and still is the most effective way of addressing the problems of humanity and effecting lasting change. And finally, the experience proved to me that at 70-plus years of age I still could learn, I still could contribute, I still could roll with the punches and survive in alien territory.

Acknowledgements

I WANT TO thank my daughter, Sigrid Cartier, my friend, Mary Bell, as well as Rachel Schumarker for taking care of my business and house during my absence which permitted me to abandon my "stuff" in the U.S. to spend time in Mali. I am also grateful to Carmen Machain-Caudill and Don Earnest for their financial support to help with mailing instructional materials to Mali and to purchase prizes for the English language competition. Particular thanks go to Hannah Cartier who developed the design for the title page, using an outline map of the country of Mali. And finally, my thanks go to friends and family members who encouraged me to make my journal available to a wider audience through publication and the very competent team at Wheatmark Publishing who made this book a reality.

Glossary

French words used in the Bambara language are annotated with (Fr). The spelling used for Bambara words is based on the Bambara dictionary in www.bambara.org/lexique/lexicon/main.htm. Special symbols are transliterated into the Latin alphabet.

Alimentation (Fr)	grocery store
Boubou	long, caftan-like attire usually worn by men
Boulangerie (Fr)	bakery
Butigi	small store that sells the necessities of life in residential neighborhoods or villages

Dugutigi	village chief (leader)
Griot (Fr)	traditional praise singer
Lycée (Fr)	secondary school
Moto	motor scooter
Muezzin (Fr)	crier/caretaker of a mosque who calls the faithful to prayer five times a day from the minaret, either live or through a recorded message by loudspeaker
Njegen	primitive outdoor toilet (enclosure with hole in floor)
Pagne (Fr)	length of cloth worn, skirt-like, generally by women; also used as blanket or curtain
Pirogue (Fr)	large, dug-out canoe
Refectoire (Fr)	dining hall
Salon (Fr)	living room

Selidaga	plastic water kettle used for toilet hygiene and ablutions
Sotrama	mini van refurbished with wooden seats for public transportation
Tubab/Tubabu	white person, European, Frenchman or woman, foreigner

Suggested Readings

Antonson, Rick. *To Timbuktu for a Haircut: A Journey through West Africa.* Toronto: The Dundurn Group, 2010.

Bingen, R. James, David Robinson, and John M. Staatz, eds. *Democracy and Development in Mali.* Ann Arbor: Michigan State University Press, 2000.

De Villiers, Marq, and Sheila Hirtle. *Timbuktu – The Sahara's Fabled City of Gold.* New York: Walker and Co., 2007.

Holloway, Kris. *Monique and the Mango Rains: Two Years with a Midwife in Mali.* Long Grove, Illinois: Waveland Press, 2007.

Kingsolver, Barbara. *The Poisonwood Bible.* New York: Perennial - HarperCollins, 1999.

Klein, Robert. *Being First: An Informal History of the Early Peace Corps.* Tucson, Arizona: Wheatmark, 2010.

Lawder, Donald. *Fishing in the Sky: The Education of Namory Keita*. Sag Harbor, New York: The Permanent Press, 1997.

Spaulding, Marcy L. *Dancing Trees and Crocodile Dreams: My Life in a West African Village*. Fresno, California: Poppy Lane Publisher, 2004.

For other publications by U.S. Peace Corps Volunteers having served in Africa or elsewhere, please see Hudson, Rex A. Annotated Bibliography of Peace Corps Writers' Books in the Library of Congress. Peace Corps 50th Anniversary, September 22, 2011. (http://www.peacecorpswriters.org/pages/depts/resources/bibliog/bib.html)

About the Author

RENATE SCHULZ WAS born in Germany and came to the United States at the age of eighteen. She holds a Ph.D. in Foreign Language Education from The Ohio State University. She retired from her professorship in the Department of German Studies at the University of Arizona in 2009, after spending almost thirty years at that institution in various academic and administrative positions. Remembering the life-changing effect of her first Peace Corps service in Nigeria between 1963 and 1965, she rejoined the U.S. Peace Corps in 2011 for what she hoped would be a 27-months sojourn in Mali, West Africa. *Life in Alien Territory* is based on the journal entries that she had shared electronically with family and friends while in Mali. She lives in Tucson, Arizona.